First World War
and Army of Occupation
War Diary
France, Belgium and Germany

36 DIVISION
Divisional Troops
121 Field Company Royal Engineers
3 October 1915 - 28 February 1919

WO95/2497/1

The Naval & Military Press Ltd
www.nmarchive.com
Published in association with The National Archives

Published by

The Naval & Military Press Ltd

Unit 10 Ridgewood Industrial Park,

Uckfield, East Sussex,

TN22 5QE England

Tel: +44 (0) 1825 749494

www.naval-military-press.com

www.nmarchive.com

This diary has been reprinted in facsimile from the original. Any imperfections are inevitably reproduced and the quality may fall short of modern type and cartographic standards.

Contents

Document type	Place/Title	Date From	Date To
Heading	WO95/2497/1 121 Field Company Royal Engineers		
Heading	36th Division 121st Field Coy R.E. Oct 1915-Feb 1919		
Heading	36th Division 121th 7.c. R.E. Vol. 1 Oct 15		
War Diary	Bordon	03/10/1915	03/10/1915
War Diary	Southampton	03/10/1915	04/10/1915
War Diary	Havre	05/10/1915	06/10/1915
War Diary	Longeau	06/10/1915	06/10/1915
War Diary	Ailly Sur Somme	07/10/1915	07/10/1915
War Diary	Ailly Sur Somme	08/10/1915	12/10/1915
War Diary	Arquires	13/10/1915	18/10/1915
War Diary	Vauchelles	19/10/1915	31/10/1915
Heading	36th Division 121th 7.c R.E. Vol : 2		
War Diary	Vauchelles	01/11/1915	01/11/1915
War Diary	Mailly Maillet	02/11/1915	07/11/1915
War Diary	Arqueves	08/11/1915	21/11/1915
War Diary	Domart	22/11/1915	27/11/1915
War Diary	Bernaville	27/11/1915	30/11/1915
Heading	36th Div 121th 7.c R.E. Vol 3		
War Diary	Monflieres	01/12/1915	31/12/1915
Heading	36th Div Jan 1916 121th 7C R.E. Vol 4		
War Diary	Monflieres	01/01/1916	08/01/1916
War Diary	Bernaville	09/01/1916	18/01/1916
War Diary	Dommesmont	19/01/1916	31/01/1916
War Diary	Dommesmont	01/02/1916	09/02/1916
War Diary	Forceville	10/02/1916	14/02/1916
War Diary	Acheux	14/02/1916	14/02/1916
War Diary	Forceville	15/02/1916	29/02/1916
Heading	121 F.C. R.E. Vol 6		
War Diary	Forceville	01/03/1916	05/03/1916
War Diary	Martinsart	06/03/1916	31/03/1916
War Diary	Martinsart	01/04/1916	30/04/1916
Miscellaneous	121st Field Coy. R.E.		
Miscellaneous	121st. Fd. Coy. R.E.		
Miscellaneous	121st. Field. Coy. R.E.		
Miscellaneous	121st. Field. Coy. R.E.	10/04/1916	10/04/1916
War Diary	Martinsart.	01/05/1916	31/05/1916
Miscellaneous	121st. Field Company. R.E. Working Parties Required For April 28th And Until Further Orders.	28/04/1916	28/04/1916
Miscellaneous	121st. Field. Coy. R.E.	28/04/1916	28/04/1916
Miscellaneous	121st Field Coy. R.E.	10/04/1916	10/04/1916
Miscellaneous			
Heading	36th Divisional Engineers 121st Field Company R.E. June 1916		
War Diary	Martinsart	01/06/1916	30/06/1916
Miscellaneous	121st Field Coy. R.E.	02/06/1916	02/06/1916
Miscellaneous	Work Tables for 121st. Field Coy. R.E. to Be Found by 10th R.I.R. Commencing 2nd June	02/06/1916	02/06/1916
Miscellaneous	Working Parties Supplied by 14th Royal List Rifles	14/06/1916	14/06/1916
Miscellaneous	Royal Engineers.		

Heading	36th Divisional Engineers. 121st Field Company R.E. July 1916		
War Diary	Martinsart	01/07/1916	01/07/1916
War Diary	Aveluy Wood	02/07/1916	02/07/1916
War Diary	Mound Keep. Q35b5.3 Ref France 57 D.S.E.	03/07/1916	04/07/1916
War Diary	Mound Keep	05/07/1916	07/07/1916
War Diary	Martinsart	08/07/1916	08/07/1916
War Diary	Harponville	09/07/1916	10/07/1916
War Diary	Beauval	11/07/1916	12/07/1916
War Diary	Serques	13/07/1916	21/07/1916
War Diary	Ledringhem	22/07/1916	22/07/1916
War Diary	St Marie-Cappel	23/07/1916	23/07/1916
War Diary	Steenwerck	24/07/1916	29/07/1916
War Diary	Romarin	30/07/1916	30/07/1916
War Diary	Romarin B4a84 France 36 N.W.	31/07/1916	05/08/1916
War Diary	Romarin	06/08/1916	31/08/1916
Miscellaneous	Weekly Progress Report 121st field Coy R.E.	23/08/1916	23/08/1916
War Diary	Le Romarin	01/09/1916	08/09/1916
War Diary	Aldershot Camp.	09/09/1916	09/09/1916
War Diary	De Kennebak.	09/09/1916	12/09/1916
War Diary	Aldershot Camp.	13/09/1916	30/09/1916
War Diary	Aldershot Camp. (T19b63 Sheet 28 S.W) Kennebak T3f 22	01/10/1916	01/10/1916
War Diary	Aldershot Camp And De Kennebak	02/10/1916	31/10/1916
War Diary	Aldershot Camp T19b63 Sheet 28 SW.	01/11/1916	01/11/1916
War Diary	De Kennebak Cabt	01/11/1916	01/11/1916
War Diary	Aldershot Camp & De Kennebak Cabt.	02/11/1916	30/11/1916
Heading	War Diary of 121st Field Company R.E. December 1916 Vol 15		
War Diary	Aldershot Camp De Kennebak Cabt	01/12/1916	31/12/1916
Heading	War Diary of O.C. 121st. Field Coy R.E. From 1/1/17 to 31/1/17. Vol 16		
War Diary	Monmouth Camp M35b44 & De Kennebak T3 Central	01/01/1917	02/01/1917
War Diary	Monmouth Camp & De Kennebak	03/01/1917	26/01/1917
War Diary	Petit Pont Form (T22b22)	27/01/1917	31/01/1917
Heading	War Diary of O.C. 121 Field Coy R.E. February 1917. Vol 17		
War Diary	Petit Pont	01/02/1917	28/02/1917
Heading	War Diary of O.C. 121 Field Coy R.E. For Month of March 1917 Vol 18		
War Diary	Petit Pont	01/03/1917	13/03/1917
War Diary	Lurgan Camp	14/03/1917	31/03/1917
Heading	War Diary of O.C. 121 field Coy. R.E. from 1st April 1917 to 30th April 1917 Vol 19		
War Diary	Lurgan Camp Bus Farm	01/04/1917	30/04/1917
Heading	War Diary of O.C. 121 field Coy R.E. for Month of May 1917. Vol 20		
War Diary	Lurgan Camp	01/05/1917	31/05/1917
Heading	War Diary of 121st Field Coy R.E. June, 1917. Vol 21		
War Diary	In The Field Lurgan Camp. Drauoutre	01/06/1917	06/06/1917
War Diary	Bus Farm	07/06/1917	08/06/1917
War Diary	Lurgan Camp	09/06/1917	14/06/1917
War Diary	N35a48	15/06/1917	16/06/1917
War Diary	N34b2.6	17/06/1917	18/06/1917
War Diary	Shamus Dugouts	19/06/1917	29/06/1917
War Diary	Watou.	30/06/1917	30/06/1917

Heading	War Diary of O.C. 121st. Field Coy. RE for Month of July 1917. Vol 22		
War Diary	Watou	01/07/1917	30/07/1917
War Diary	L16a 2.6	31/07/1917	31/07/1917
Heading	War Diary of 121st Field Company R.E. for Month of August. 1917 Vol 23		
War Diary	27L16a2.6	01/08/1917	03/08/1917
War Diary	28la37	04/08/1917	18/08/1917
War Diary	27J1d.90	19/08/1917	23/08/1917
War Diary	57CO16d09	24/08/1917	27/08/1917
War Diary	Metz	28/08/1917	31/08/1917
Heading	War Diary of 121st Field Coy R.E. for Month of September 1917 Vol 24		
War Diary	Metz	01/09/1917	30/09/1917
Heading	War Diary of 121st Field Coy RE for Month of October 1917 Vol 25		
War Diary		01/10/1917	31/10/1917
Heading	War Diary of 121st Field Company R.E. for Month of November 1917 Vol 26		
War Diary	Metz	01/11/1917	18/11/1917
War Diary	Havrincourt Wood	19/11/1917	22/11/1917
War Diary	Hermies	23/11/1917	28/11/1917
War Diary	Gomiecourt	29/11/1917	29/11/1917
War Diary	Courcelles	30/11/1917	30/11/1917
Heading	War Diary of 121st Field Coy RE for December 1917 Vol 27		
War Diary	Beaulencourt	01/12/1917	01/12/1917
War Diary	Lechelle	02/12/1917	03/12/1917
War Diary	Dessart Wood	04/12/1917	04/12/1917
War Diary	Metz	05/12/1917	14/12/1917
War Diary	Manancourt	15/12/1917	16/12/1917
War Diary	Beaudricourt	17/12/1917	26/12/1917
War Diary	Warfusee-Abancourt	27/12/1917	31/12/1917
Heading	War Diary of 121st Field Coy. R.E. for Jany. 1918 Vol 28		
War Diary	Warfusee Abancourt	01/01/1918	06/01/1918
War Diary	Framerville	07/01/1918	08/01/1918
War Diary	Voyennes	09/01/1918	10/01/1918
War Diary	Dury	11/01/1918	13/01/1918
War Diary	Hamel	14/01/1918	31/01/1918
Heading	War Diary of O.C. 121st Field Coy R.E. for Month of February 1918 Vol 29		
War Diary		01/02/1918	28/02/1918
Heading	War Diary of 121st Field Company RE for Month of March 1918 Vol 30		
War Diary	Le Hamel	01/03/1918	31/03/1918
Heading	36th Divisional Engineers 121st Field Company R.E. April 1918		
Heading	War Diary of 121 Field Coy RE for Month of April 1918 Vol 31		
Miscellaneous			
War Diary		01/04/1918	30/04/1918
Heading	War Diary of 121 Field Company RE From 1-5-18 to 31-5-18 Vol 32		
War Diary		01/05/1918	31/05/1918

Heading	War Diary of 121st Field Company RE 1-6-18 to 30-6-18 Vol 33		
War Diary		01/06/1918	30/06/1918
Heading	War Diary of 121st Field Company RE From 1-7-18 to 31-7-18 Vol 34		
War Diary		01/07/1918	31/07/1918
Heading	War Diary. 121st Field Company R.E. 1st to 31st August 1918 Vol 35		
War Diary		01/08/1918	31/08/1918
Heading	War Diary of 121st Field Company RE from 1-9-18 to 30-9-18 Vol 36		
War Diary		01/09/1918	30/09/1918
Heading	War Diary for Month of October, 1918. 121st Field Coy R.E. Vol 37		
War Diary		01/10/1918	31/10/1918
War Diary	121st field Co R.E. War Diary for Month of Nov. 1918 Vol 38		
War Diary		01/11/1918	30/11/1918
Heading	War Diary of 121 Field Company-RE for December. 1918 Vol 39		
War Diary		01/12/1918	31/12/1918
War Diary	War Diary of 121 Field Company RE for January. 1919 Vol 40		
War Diary		01/01/1919	31/01/1919
War Diary	War Diary of 121 Field Company R.E. for February 1919 Vol 41		
War Diary	Field	01/02/1919	28/02/1919

WO 195/2497/1

121 Field Company Royal Engineers

36TH DIVISION

121ST FIELD COY R.E.

OCT 1915-FEB 1919

36th Division

121
7592

121st F. C. R. E.
Vol: I

Oct 15

Instructions regarding War Diaries and Intelligence Summaries are contained in F. S. Regs., Part II. and the Staff Manual respectively. Title pages will be prepared in manuscript.

WAR DIARY of 121st. Field Coy. R.E. 36th (Ulster) Division
~~INTELLIGENCE SUMMARY.~~

(*Erase heading not required.*)

Army Form C. 2118.

Place	Date	Hour	Summary of Events and Information	Remarks and references to Appendices
Bordon	3.10.15	9.30 p.m.	1st half of Coy. entrained at Bordon	
		11 p.m.	2nd " " " " C. Craig	
Southampton	"	11.30 p.m.	1st half of Coy detrained at Southampton	
	4.10.15	1 a.m.	2nd " " "	
	"	4 p.m.	whole Coy sailed from Southampton on S.S. City of Benares C. Craig	
Havre	5.10.15	6 a.m.	" disembarked. ~~Interpreter~~	
		12 noon	" arrived at No 5 rest Camp Interpreter joined us here The weather has been very bad today – rain for the greater part of the day & night C. Craig	
"	6.10.15	10 a.m.	Coy. entrained at point 3. Train departed 1.19 p.m. C. Craig	
Longeau	"	11.15 p.m.	Coy detrained & proceeded to march (transport accompanying us) to Ailly sur Somme a distance of 11 K. C. Craig	
Ailly sur Somme	7.10.15	5 a.m.	Coy arrived Ailly sur Somme & breakfasted With the help of our interpreter billets without subsistence were secured for the Coy. in a large hall belonging to the jute mill. This mill is owned by a gentleman of English extraction, his grandfather being English C. Craig	

2353 Wt. W2544/1454 700,000 5/15 D. D. & L. A.D.S.S./Forms/C. 2118.

Army Form C. [illegible]8.

Instructions regarding War Diaries and Intelligence Summaries are contained in F. S. Regs., Part II. and the Staff Manual respectively. Title pages will be prepared in manuscript.

V/

WAR DIARY
of 121st Field Coy. R.E.

~~INTELLIGENCE SUMMARY~~. 36th (Ulster) Division.

(Erase heading not required.)

Place	Date	Hour	Summary of Events and Information	Remarks and references to Appendices
Ailly-sur-Somme.	8.10.15		The day was spent in overhauling our general equipment, & building shelters. Weather fine. Our interpreter Monsieur Cambulzier took his place. C.C. v. a	
"	9.10.15		The work of building shelters was proceeded with & we had a short Route March in the afternoon – weather continues to be fine.	
"	10.10.15		(Sunday) – Clothing Inspection – weather fine. C.C.	
"	11.10.15		one hours musketry drill in the morning with section route march in forenoon. In the afternoon lecture on musketry & search lights by Captn Otway	
"	12.10.15		Coy. moved from Ailly sur Somme to ~~Arch~~ Arquieves marching via Amiens, Contay & Toutencourt. Left Ailly 9.45 a.m. arrived Arquieves 7.30 p.m. (24 miles march) C.C.	
Arquieves	13.10.15		Day spent in laying out Camp, digging latrines etc. C.C.	

2353 Wt. W2544/1454 700,000 5/15 D. D. & L. A.D.S.S./Forms/C. 2118.

3/

Army Form C. 2118.

Instructions regarding War Diaries and Intelligence Summaries are contained in F. S. Regs., Part II. and the Staff Manual respectively. Title pages will be prepared in manuscript.

WAR DIARY
or
INTELLIGENCE SUMMARY.
(Erase heading not required.)

Place	Date	Hour	Summary of Events and Information	Remarks and references to Appendices
Arquèves	14.10.15		Coy. employed in Trench digging in the neighbourhood ~~Dis~~ Mounted men excercise their horses - drill C.C	
"	15.10.15		do C.C.	
"	16.10.15		do C.C.	
"	17.10.15		Arm & Kit Inspection - lecture on Gas helmets (Tube pattern) by R.F. M.O. ~~Emergency~~ Iron rations issued Inspection of Camp by C.R.E. C.C	
"	18.10.15		Coy moved to VAUCHELLES. Left ARQEVES 10 a.m. arrived Vauchelles 11 a.m. In the afternoon tents were pitched horses & mules picketed & latrines dug C.C	
Vauchelles	19.10.15		Coy employed at ~~Trench digging~~ Laying out Trenches in the neighbourhood working under instructions received from C.R.E. 36th Div. C.C	
	20.10.15		do C.C.	
	21.10.15		do C.C.	

4/

Instructions regarding War Diaries and Intelligence Summaries are contained in F. S. Regs., Part II. and the Staff Manual respectively. Title pages will be prepared in manuscript.

WAR DIARY or INTELLIGENCE SUMMARY.

(*Erase heading not required.*)

121st Field Coy R.E.

Army Form C. 2118.

Place	Date	Hour	Summary of Events and Information	Remarks and references to Appendices
Vauchelles	22/10/15		same as 21-10-15 - nights cold & frosty days fine with plenty of sun	C.C.
	23/10/15		do "	C.C.
	24/10/15		(Sunday) Pay parade & kit inspection - weather wet.	C.C.
	25/10/15		Continuation of marking out defence works	C.C.
	26/10/15		do	C.C.
	27/10/15		do also packing up in anticipation of move. Officers & Senior N.C.O.s spent 2 hours marking out defence works at night - weather wet one man transferred to 4 casualty clearing station - off strength from this date	C.C.
	28/10/15		marking out defence works continued weather stormy another man transferred to 4 casualty clearing station - off strength from this date	
	29/10/15		do	C.C.
	30/10/15		do "	C.C.
	31/10/15		(Sunday) preparation for move	C.C.

2353 Wt. W2544/1454 700,000 5/15 D. D. & L. A.D.S.S./Forms/C. 2118.

36th Division

121st F.C.R.E.
Vol: 2

121/7678

Nov 15

5/

Instructions regarding War Diaries and Intelligence Summaries are contained in F. S. Regs., Part II. and the Staff Manual respectively. Title pages will be prepared in manuscript.

WAR DIARY of ~~INTELLIGENCE SUMMARY~~. 121st Field Coy. R.E.

(*Erase heading not required.*)

Army Form C. 2118

Place	Date	Hour	Summary of Events and Information	Remarks and references to Appendices
Vauchelles	1-11-15		Coy with the exception of 6 men + 7 horses who were temporarily attached to 150th Fd Coy. at ARQUEVES moved to MAILLY-MAILLET marching via LOUVENCOURT, ACHEUX + FORCEVILLE on reaching the latter place the sections proceeded at ten minutes interval. The roads were very dirty bad especially from ACHEUX. Nos 2 + 4 sections under Captn Olivay continued the march to ENGLEBELMER + were attached West Lancs Fd Coy. R.E. for instructional purposes. The remaining sections at MAILLY were attached 9th Fd. Coy. R.E. for a similar purpose. Rain was continuous throughout the day. The billets are mere hovels. CC.	
MAILLY-MAILLET	2-11-15		Heavy Rain continues. No 1 + 3 section ~~had~~ their first experience of the ~~2nd~~ line trenches. They were up having a general survey + getting some work in connection with repairs of some of the trenches alloted to them. CC.	

2353 Wt. W2544/1454 700,000 5/15 D. D. & L. A.D.S.S./Forms/C. 2118.

6

Instructions regarding War Diaries and Intelligence Summaries are contained in F. S. Regs., Part II. and the Staff Manual respectively. Title pages will be prepared in manuscript.

WAR DIARY of ~~INTELLIGENCE SUMMARY~~. 121st Fd. Coy. R.E.

(Erase heading not required.)

Army Form C. 2118.

Place	Date	Hour	Summary of Events and Information	Remarks and references to Appendices
Mailly-maillet	3-11-15		French work in 2nd line - repairing trenches. - weather still bad one section works in day time - the other from 4.30 p.m. to 11 p.m. ditto for sections at ENGLEBELMER	
	4-11-15		do	
	5-11-15		do - weather not quite so bad	
	6-11-15		do - day moderately fine	
	7-11-15	(Sun)	Coy returned to ARQUEVES - left MAILLY-MAILLET 9 a.m. arrived ARQUEVES 12 ~~midday~~. Later in the day Nos 1 + 3 Sections proceeded to VAUCHELLES + were billeted there	C.C.
ARQUEVES	8-11-15		French work - laying out defensive positions. Nos 1 + 3 do. - also repairing billets	C.C.
	9-11-15		do. weather comparatively mild	C.C.
	10-11-15		do	C.C.
	11-11-15		No 4 section moved into billets at CANDAS	C.C.
	12-11-15		Defensive works continued	C.C.
	13-11-15		"	C.C.

2353 Wt. W2544/1454 700,000 5/15 D. D. & L. A.D.S.S./Forms/C. 2118.

7

Instructions regarding War Diaries and Intelligence Summaries are contained in F. S. Regs., Part II. and the Staff Manual respectively. Title pages will be prepared in manuscript.

WAR DIARY or ~~INTELLIGENCE SUMMARY~~. 1/2 1st Field Coy R.E.

(*Erase heading not required.*)

Army Form C. 2118.

Place	Date	Hour	Summary of Events and Information	Remarks and references to Appendices
ARQUEVES	14/11/15		(Sun). HQ ~~Sectns~~ marched VAUCHELLES for baths. - inspection of transport by O.C.	C.C.
	15/11/15		Work on defensive positions - Some snow fell during the night	C.C.
	16/11/15		" Snow continues	C.C.
	17/11/15		" " with frost at night.	C.C.
	18/11/15		" night now frosty & cold	C.C.
	19/11/15		" "	C.C.
	20/11/15		" "	C.C.
	21/11/15		(Sun). Left ARQUEVES 9.45 a.m. arrived DOMART-en-PONTHIEU 5 p.m. & were billetted there.	C.C.
DOMART	22/11/15		The distribution of the sections now is H.Q. & No 2 sections at DOMART Nos 1 & 3 at VAUCHELLES No 4 Section at CANDAS.	C.C.

2353 Wt. W2544/1454 700,000 5/15 D. D. & L. A.D.S.S./Forms/C. 2118.

8/

Instructions regarding War Diaries and Intelligence Summaries are contained in F. S. Regs., Part II. and the Staff Manual respectively. Title pages will be prepared in manuscript.

WAR DIARY
or
~~INTELLIGENCE~~ SUMMARY.
(Erase heading not required.)

97?1st Field Coy. R.E.

Army Form C. 2118.

Place	Date	Hour	Summary of Events and Information	Remarks and references to Appendices
DOMART	23/11/15		Transport overhauled. cleaned wheels greased etc. weather mild	CE
	24/11/15		General Fatigue work in billets "	CE
	25/11/15		No. 2 section moved into billets at ~~COCQUEREL~~ PONT-REMY. This leaves only H.Q. sect. at DOMART.	CE
	26/11/15		Preparation for moving.	CE
	27/11/15		H.Q. section with personnel proceeded to BERNAVILLE billeting for the night. No 1 + 3 sections also moved from VAUCHELLES les AUTHIE here. Heavy frost at night.	CE
BERNAVILLE	28/11/15		All sections moved into billets at MOUFLIERS. Sections left BERNAVILLE 9 am. arrived MOUFLIERS 3.30 p.m.	CE
	29/11/15		arranging + cleaning billets - very wet.	CE
	30/11/15		do also making paths. - one section employed in marking out trenches for instructional purposes beside the village.	CE

9/

Instructions regarding War Diaries and Intelligence Summaries are contained in F. S. Regs., Part II. and the Staff Manual respectively. Title pages will be prepared in manuscript.

WAR DIARY ~~or INTELLIGENCE SUMMARY.~~

(Erase heading not required.)

212th Field Coy. R.E.

Army Form C. 2118.

Place	Date	Hour	Summary of Events and Information	Remarks and references to Appendices
MONFLIERES	1/12/15		Repairs to Billets + general cleaning - wet day	CC
	2/12/15		one section Pontooning at PONTREMY another wood cutting at BUSSUS remainder repairing billets	CC
	3/12/15		do do	CC
	4/12/15		do do	CC
	5/12/15		(Sunday) washing vehicles - Rifle inspection - issuing Comforts Pay parade	CC
	6/12/15		one section Pontooning remainder woodcutting + billet repairs. Circular saw (portable) + engine brought from ABBEVILLE for sawing wood for Division	CC
	7/12		Pontooning + woodcutting - overhauling engine.	CC

2353 Wt. W2544/1454 700,000 5/15 D. D. & L. A.D.S.S./Forms/C. 2118.

10

Instructions regarding War Diaries and Intelligence Summaries are contained in F. S. Regs., Part II. and the Staff Manual respectively. Title pages will be prepared in manuscript.

WAR DIARY

or

~~INTELLIGENCE SUMMARY.~~

(*Erase heading not required.*)

of 121st Field Coy R.E.

Army Form C. 2118.

Place	Date	Hour	Summary of Events and Information	Remarks and references to Appendices
MONFLIERES	8/12/15		Woodcutting at BUSSUS - repairing billets 10 men sent to supervise horse standings for 36th Divisional Artillery	CC
"	9/12/15		Pontooning at EAUCOURT Felling timber at BUSSUS repairing billets MONFLIERES. - squad + rifle drill.	CC
"	10/12/15		do + arranging sawmill	CC
			+ Inoculation for some men by M.O.	CC
"	11/12/15		do	
"	12/12/15		Inspection of billets by O.C. Foot, kit + rifle inspection Church parades.	CC
"	13/12/15		Felling timber at EAUCOURT - sawing timber at BUSSUS Pontooning at EAUCOURT.	CC

2353 Wt. W2544/1454 700,000 5/15 D. D. & L. A.D.S.S. Forms/C. 2118.

Instructions regarding War Diaries and Intelligence Summaries are contained in F. S. Regs., Part II. and the Staff Manual respectively. Title pages will be prepared in manuscript.

11

WAR DIARY
or
~~INTELLIGENCE SUMMARY~~.
(Erase heading not required.)

1210 Field Coy R.E.

Army Form C. 2118.

Place	Date	Hour	Summary of Events and Information	Remarks and references to Appendices
MONFLIERES	14 12 15		Pontooning at EAUCOURT – Sawing timber at BUSSUS remainder 1 hour squad drill + instructing Infantry in Field works including revetting wire netting (lecture by M.O. on 1st Aid)	CC
"	15 12		do with exception of lecture	CC
"	16 12		do "	CC
"	17 12		do "	CC
"	18 12		do "	CC
"	19 12		(Sunday) washing vehicles – kit rifle + foot inspection.	R CC
"	20 12		Pontooning at EAUCOURT – Same as Mon (14th) ~~sections~~ (48 men) at a time	CC
"	21 12		do	CC

2353 Wt. W2544/1454 700,000 5/15 D. D. & L. A.D.S.S. Forms/C. 2118.

12/

WAR DIARY

~~or~~

~~INTELLIGENCE SUMMARY.~~ 121st Field Coy R.E.

(Erase heading not required.)

Army Form C. 2118.

Instructions regarding War Diaries and Intelligence Summaries are contained in F. S. Regs., Part II. and the Staff Manual respectively. Title pages will be prepared in manuscript.

Place	Date	Hour	Summary of Events and Information	Remarks and references to Appendices
MONFLIERES	22/12/15		Pontooning at EAUCOURT (same men for 3 days). - remainder 1 hr. Squad drill & instructing Infantry 108 Bde in revetting wire entanglements etc	CC
	23/12/15		do	CC
	24/12/15		do men on detachment supervising horse standings for R.A. return also men working saw mill at BUSSUS	CC
	25/12		XMAS day. - Holiday - Football in afternoon (Church parades in the morning). Xmas enjoyed very much by all ranks Extras were provided from our Canteen fund. Large amounts were also received & very much appreciated by the men from Ulster Women's Gift Fund Belfast	CC
	26/12		(Sunday) Holiday	CC
	27/12		Repairs to billets up to 12.45 pm. - Holiday for remainder of day	CC

13

Instructions regarding War Diaries and Intelligence Summaries are contained in F. S. Regs., Part II. and the Staff Manual respectively. Title pages will be prepared in manuscript.

WAR DIARY
or
~~INTELLIGENCE SUMMARY~~.

of 121st Field Coy R.E.

(Erase heading not required.)

Army Form C. 2118.

Place	Date	Hour	Summary of Events and Information	Remarks and references to Appendices
MONFLIERES	28/12/15		Field works + instructing detachments of Infantry in revetting, wire entanglements etc. Saw mill working at BUSSUS. CC	
	29/12/15		do CC	
	30/12/15		do CC	
	31/12/15		do CC	

C Craig Major
O.C. 121st R.E. Field Co

2353 Wt. W2544/1454 700,000 5/15 D. D. & L. A.D.S.S./Forms/C. 2118.

121st F.C.R.E.

Vol 4

36th Div Jan 1916

14

Instructions regarding War Diaries and Intelligence Summaries are contained in F. S. Regs., Part II. and the Staff Manual respectively. Title pages will be prepared in manuscript.

WAR DIARY
~~or~~
~~INTELLIGENCE SUMMARY~~. of 121st Field Coy. R.E.

(Erase heading not required.)

Army Form C. 2118.

Place	Date	Hour	Summary of Events and Information	Remarks and references to Appendices
MONFLIERES	1/6/16		Instructions received from C.R.E. that Coy would shortly move to LANCHES. The portable saw working at BUSSUS was sent to LANCHES – ~~[illegible]~~ Pontoon wagons overhauled + washed. 1 NCO + 2 men sent to CANAPLES to take over R.E. workshop.	C.C.
"	2/6/16		(Sunday) General cleaning of Billets. Church parades + Pay parade	C.C.
"	3/6/16		Advance party of 1 N.C.O. + 3 men sent to LANCHES to take over billets from 208th Field Coy. R.E. also 2 loads of stores sent, wagons to return next day. Party of 1 N.C.O. + 9 men sent to bring Portable engine ~~saw~~ from BUSSUS to LANCHES. Motor lorry brought saw bench (stationary) from MONFLIERES to LANCHES. Party of cyclists sent to unload it there. No 4 Section with its transport + equipment proceeded to CANDAS to take over R.E. workshop there.	C.C.

2353 Wt. W2544/1454 700,000 5/15 D. D. & L. A.D.S.S. Forms/C. 2118.

15

Army Form C. 2118.

Instructions regarding War Diaries and Intelligence Summaries are contained in F. S. Regs., Part II. and the Staff Manual respectively. Title pages will be prepared in manuscript.

WAR DIARY of 121st Field Coy R.E.

~~or INTELLIGENCE SUMMARY.~~

(Erase heading not required.)

Place	Date	Hour	Summary of Events and Information	Remarks and references to Appendices
MONFLIERES	4/1/16		Party sent with saw to LANCHES return. General fatigues + repairing of damage done to Billets. Party at Field works CC	
"	5/1/16		do do - weather has been fine recently. CC	
"	6/1/16		do Party at Field Works CC	
"	7/1/16		Repairing Billets - General Repairs. Party loading stores at R.E. Stores CANDAS Orders received to move to BERNAVILLE CC	
"	~~8/1/16~~ 8/1/16		HQrs + No 2 section ~~Coy~~ marched to BERNAVILLE No 1 section to HALLOY CC No 3 section to OUTREBOIS. Coy was divided up in this manner to superintend works in connection with new "hutting scheme". This scheme was to provide ~~[illegible]~~ increased accomodation for troops + also improve existing billets. Beds made with wire netting are being provided CC	

2353 Wt. W2544/1454 700,000 5/15 D. D. & L. A.D.S.S. Forms/C 2118.

16

Instructions regarding War Diaries and Intelligence Summaries are contained in F. S. Regs., Part II. and the Staff Manual respectively. Title pages will be prepared in manuscript.

WAR DIARY
or
~~INTELLIGENCE SUMMARY~~ of 121st Field Coy. R.E.

(Erase heading not required.)

Army Form C. 2118.

Place	Date	Hour	Summary of Events and Information	Remarks and references to Appendices
BERNAVILLE	9.1.16		General cleaning of new billets. Orders received to start an R.E. store to supply timber nails wire netting etc to works officer on Hutting scheme.	CC
"	10/1/16		Cleaning of Billets - drawing stores from LANCHES + CANDAS	CC
"	11/1/16		" + repairs to Billets	CC
"	12/1/16		" " + Issuing timber etc from R.E. Stores here	CC
"	13/1/16		do do	CC
"	14/1/16		do do Timber received for Reserve from sawmill at LONGVILLERS	CC
"	15/1/16		do do	CC
"	16/1/16		do do Orders received to move	CC
"	17/1/16		do do to DOMMESMONT - Stores were being drawn to this place on 16th + 17th. Distance from BERNAVILLE 2.8 K	CC
"	18/1/16		H.Q. + No 2 Section moved to DOMMESMONT. Stores being moved all the day	CC

17

Instructions regarding War Diaries and Intelligence Summaries are contained in F. S. Regs., Part II. and the Staff Manual respectively. Title pages will be prepared in manuscript.

WAR DIARY
or
~~INTELLIGENCE SUMMARY.~~

(Erase heading not required.)

of 121st Field Coy RE

Army Form C. 2118.

Place	Date	Hour	Summary of Events and Information	Remarks and references to Appendices
DOMMESMONT.	19/1/16		Cleaning of Billets & Repairs to same in accordance with Hutting Scheme. Issuing timber etc from stores.	CC
"	20/1/16		do do	CC
"	21/1/16		do do	CC
"	22/1/16		do do	CC
"	23/1/16		(Sunday) Kit Inspection Inspection of Gas Helmets Bathing Church Parades.	CC
"	24/1/16		Repairs to Billets - making beds in accordance with Hutting scheme	CC
"	25/1/16		do do	CC
"	26/1/16		Brought portable engine from LANCHES part of the way to ABBEVILLE - Billets improvements	CC
"	27/1/16		Party proceeded to ABBEVILLE with portable engine billeting for the night at MONFLIERES & returning next day.	CC
"	28/1/16		Saw bench from LANCHES brought to CANDAS. Billet improvement at DOMMESMONT	CC
"	29/1/16		Repair & improvement of Billets. Weather has been fairly good recently.	CC

2353 Wt. W2544/1454 700,000 5/15 D. D. & L. A.D.S.S. Forms/C. 2118.

Instructions regarding War Diaries and Intelligence Summaries are contained in F. S. Regs. Part II. and the Staff Manual respectively. Title pages will be prepared in manuscript.

18/

WAR DIARY of 121st Field Coy. R.E.

~~INTELLIGENCE SUMMARY.~~

(Erase heading not required.)

Army Form C. 2118.

Place	Date	Hour	Summary of Events and Information	Remarks and references to Appendices
DOMMESMONT	30-4-16		(Sunday). Church Parades. Gas Helmet Inspections + issue of replacements of those unserviceable. Issue of Sheepskin Coats. Orders were received for movements of units of 108 Bde to which we are attached. These were cancelled at 10.30 pm. CC	
"	31/5/16		Making Horse troughs. Storing saw bench at LANCHES + repairing + improvement of billets. CC	

C Craig ......Major, R.E.
O.C. 121st Field Coy., R.E.

2353 Wt. W2544/1454 700,000 5/15 D. D. & L. A.D.S.S./Forms/C 2118.

Instructions regarding War Diaries and Intelligence Summaries are contained in F. S. Regs., Part II. and the Staff Manual respectively. Title pages will be prepared in manuscript.

19

WAR DIARY
or
~~INTELLIGENCE SUMMARY.~~
(Erase heading not required.)

121st Field Coy R.E.

Army Form C. 2118.

Place	Date	Hour	Summary of Events and Information	Remarks and references to Appendices
DOMMESMONT	1.2.16		No 1 section marched from HALLOY-LES-PERNOIS to DOMMESMONT there to be billeted	ee
"	2.2.16		Erecting beds under Hutting scheme	ee
"	3.2.16		do + general improvement of billets	ee
"	4.2.16		General improvement of billets	ee
"	5.2.16		do	ee
"	6.2.16		(Sunday) Foot kit + Gas helmet Inspection	ee
"	7.2.16		Packing of wagons in view of move on 9th.	ee
"	8.2.16		do. No 4 section moved from CANDAS to FORCEVILLE.	ee
"	9.2.16		No 3 section moved from OUTREBOIS to FORCEVILLE HQ + No 1 section moved from DOMMESMONT to FORCEVILLE Left DOMMESMONT 8.0 a.m. arrived FORCEVILLE 5.30 p.m. marched via BERNAVILLE, BERNUEIL, MONTRELIET BEAUSQUESNE RAINCHEVAL ARQUEVES LEALVILLERS + ACHEUX	ee

20

Instructions regarding War Diaries and Intelligence Summaries are contained in F. S. Regs., Part II. and the Staff Manual respectively. Title pages will be prepared in manuscript.

WAR DIARY
of 121st Field Coy R.E.
~~INTELLIGENCE SUMMARY.~~

(Erase heading not required.)

Army Form C. 2118.

Place	Date	Hour	Summary of Events and Information	Remarks and references to Appendices
FORCEVILLE			General repair to billets + erecting beds (wire) for men	
"	10.2.16			C.C.
"	11.2.16		do do	C.C.
"	12.2.16		do 40 men working on	
"			Horse standings which are very urgently reqd	C.C.
"	13.2.16		(Sunday) Horse standings to 12.30 pm. Pay parade	C.C.
"	14.2.16		Horse standings	C.C.
ACHEUX	"		Erecting baths at Sucrerie - working engine for pumping water	
FORCEVILLE			Repairs to Billets + horse standings. Erecting baths at	C.C.
	15.2.16		ACHEUX (17 men) Engine drivers + sawyers at ACHEUX (7)	C.C.
"	16.2.16		do	C.C.
"	17.2.16		do do	C.C.
"	18.2.16		do do but baths completed	C.C.
"	19.2.16		do do	C.C.
"	20.2.16		(Sunday) do do Heavy bombardment lasting for 1½ hours was heard in the evening 6 - 7.30 pm.	C.C.
"	21.2.16		do do	
			Running of Engine for water supply taken over by 230th Fort Coy R.E.	C.C.

2353 Wt. W2544/1454 700,000 5/15 D. D. & L. A.D.S.S. Forms/C. 2118.

21

Instructions regarding War Diaries and Intelligence Summaries are contained in F. S. Regs., Part II. and the Staff Manual respectively. Title pages will be prepared in manuscript.

WAR DIARY or ~~INTELLIGENCE~~ SUMMARY.

of 121st Field Coy R.E.

(Erase heading not required.)

Army Form C. 2118.

Place	Date	Hour	Summary of Events and Information	Remarks and references to Appendices
FORCEVILLE	22/2/16		Horse standings & repairs to billets	C.C.
"	23/2/16		do do Some snow during the afternoon	C.C.
"	24/2/16		do do Heavy frost night 23/2/16/24/2/16 orders received that the Coy will move shortly further back from the front line.	C.C.
"	25/2/16		Cleaning of wagons & horse standings. Lt. Harrison proceeded to AUTHICULE to join Rly Coy there.	C.C.
"	26/2/16		Cleaning of wagons (difficult owing to frost) 100 men bathed at the 36th Divisional Baths in the forenoon & remainder of Coy in the afternoon – frost continues	C.C.
"	27/2/16		(Sunday) Work in forenoon on Horse standings. Afternoon issues of Clothing. "Thaw" scheme came into force today.	C.C.
"			Rations drawn from DOULLENS.	C.C.
"	28/2/16		Horse standings & repairs to billets. Repairs to Sucrerie ACHEUX	C.C.
"	29/2/16		do do	C.C.

C. Craig Major
O.C. 121st R.E.C.

2353 Wt. W2544/1454 700,000 5/15 D. D. & L. A.D.S.S./Forms/C. 2118.

22

Instructions regarding War Diaries and Intelligence Summaries are contained in F. S. Regs., Part II. and the Staff Manual respectively. Title pages will be prepared in manuscript.

WAR DIARY or ~~INTELLIGENCE~~ SUMMARY.

of 121st Field Coy R.E.

(Erase heading not required.)

Army Form C. 2118.

Place	Date	Hour	Summary of Events and Information	Remarks and references to Appendices
FORCEVILLE	1-3-16		Repairs to billets - Horsestandings - Packing of Pontoon wagons in the afternoon in anticipation of an early move	CC
"	2-3-16		Repairs to Billets + Horsestandings - men bathed at baths ACHEUX.	CC
"	3-3-16		Pontoons brought to new R.E Park South of HEDAUVILLE. wagons with 2 GS wagons remove R.E stores of 48th Div from SENLIS to this park. Repairs to Billets - Four sappers sent to take over pumping engines in new area	CC
"	4-3-16		Repairs to billets - Parties working at new RE park ACHEUX also building shed for 108th Fd Ambl. FORCEVILLE.	CC
"	5-3-16		Coy having received orders moved (less No 3 section) to MARTINSART there to be billeted.	CC
MARTINSART	6-3-16		General work at billets principally in rearranging RE stores etc	CC
"	7-3-16		Party shellproofing pumping station + well " removing R.E. stores from FORCEVILLE to MARTINSART. " rearranging R.E. store No 3 section moved from FORCEVILLE to MESNIL	CC

23

Instructions regarding War Diaries and Intelligence Summaries are contained in F. S. Regs., Part II. and the Staff Manual respectively. Title pages will be prepared in manuscript.

WAR DIARY or ~~INTELLIGENCE~~ SUMMARY. of 121st Field Coy R.E.

(Erase heading not required.)

Army Form C. 2118.

Place	Date	Hour	Summary of Events and Information	Remarks and references to Appendices
MARTINSART	8/3/16		Bomb proofing, engine house, drawing R.E. stores from HEDAUVILLE Removing "Elephants" to AUTHILLE. Rearranging R.E. stores Lt. C. of M. N. Ryan. R.E. (SR) reported for duty	CC
"	9/3/16		Party bomb proofing engine house " Drawing stores from HEDAUVILLE to R.E. stores MARTINSART. 3 parties of 9. 5 & 5 making bomb stores & dugouts at GORDON CASTLE	CC
"	10/3/16		Removing stores from MAILLY to R.E. stores MARTINSART. Parties assisted by parties of Infantry working on dugouts & bomb stores at AUTHUILLE Gordon Castle, Paisley Av. Elgin Av. & Wade Lane General work R.E. stores.	CC
"	11/3/16		Removing stores from MAILLY to R.E. stores Party general work at R.E. stores Parties assisted by Infantry working on dug-outs as on 10th	CC
"	12/3/16		do do do.	CC

2353 Wt. W2544/1454 700,000 5/15 D. D. & L. A.D.S.S./Forms/C. 2118.

Instructions regarding War Diaries and Intelligence Summaries are contained in F. S. Regs., Part II. and the Staff Manual respectively. Title pages will be prepared in manuscript.

24

WAR DIARY
of 121st Field Coy RE
~~INTELLIGENCE SUMMARY.~~
(*Erase heading not required.*)

Army Form C. 2118.

Place	Date	Hour	Summary of Events and Information	Remarks and references to Appendices
MARTINSART	13/3/16		Party drawing R.E. stores from MAILLY - Part transport provided by 109 Bde.	
			" of 8 assisted by 30 Infantry making dug outs AUTHUILLE	
			" of 13 " 40 " " GORDON CASTLE.	
			" 5 " 10 " Bomb stores "	
			6 " 20 " dug outs ~~ELGIN~~ PAISLEY	
			10 " 20 " " " av.	CC
			" 13 - - - - - " WADE LANE	
			Remainder General carpentry work	
"	14/3/16		do do	CC
"	15/3/16		do do	CC
"	16/3/16		do do	CC
"	17/3/16		Party assisted by Infantry bombproofing Engine house MARTINSART	
			Parties assisted by Infantry on Dug-outs + Bombstores GORDON CASTLE	
			PAISLEY AV., ELGIN AV. WADE LANE	CC
			Drawing R.E. stores from MAILLY - (52176) CSM. Mew C. slightly wounded by shrapnel in MARTINSART.	
"	~~18/3/16~~			

T2134. Wt. W708—776. 500000. 4/15. Sir J. C. & S.

25

Instructions regarding War Diaries and Intelligence Summaries are contained in F. S. Regs., Part II. and the Staff Manual respectively. Title pages will be prepared in manuscript.

WAR DIARY or ~~INTELLIGENCE SUMMARY~~ of 121st Field Coy. R.E.

(Erase heading not required.)

Army Form C. 2118.

Place	Date	Hour	Summary of Events and Information	Remarks and references to Appendices
MARTINSART	18/3/16		Parties assisted by Infantry working on Bombstores + dug outs at GORDON CASTLE, PAISLEY AV. ELGIN AV + WADE LANE Bombproofing pumping Engine MARTINSART. Drawing R.E. stores from MAILLY No 64162 LCpl. Orr S. wounded No 64075 Sapper Caughley P. severely wounded 2nd Lieut. J.A. Wilson R.E. reported for duty.	CC
"	19/3/16		do do	CC
"	20/3/16		do do 64075 Sapper Caughley P. died from wounds.	CC
"	21/3/16		Parties assisted by Infantry 9th R. Innis Fus working on Bombstore dugouts at GORDON CASTLE, PAISLEY AV. ELGIN AV. + WADE LANE Bomb proofing pumping engine MARTINSART Drawing R.E. stores from MAILLY.	CC
"	22/3/16		do do do	CC
"	23/3/16		do do do Infantry found by 9th + 11th R. Innis Fus.	CC

T2134. Wt. W708—776. 500000. 4/15. Sir J. C. & S.

26

Instructions regarding War Diaries and Intelligence Summaries are contained in F. S. Regs., Part II. and the Staff Manual respectively. Title pages will be prepared in manuscript.

WAR DIARY or ~~INTELLIGENCE SUMMARY~~. of 121st Field Coy R.E.

(Erase heading not required.)

Army Form C. 2118.

Place	Date	Hour	Summary of Events and Information	Remarks and references to Appendices
MARTINSART	24/3/16		The making of Dug-outs at GORDON CASTLE, PAISLEY AV. ELGIN AV. WADE LANE BROMIELAW ST still continues. Infantry Parties supplied by 9th + 11th R. In. Fus. Maintenance of JACOB'S LADDER is supervised by Lt. Ferries (No 3 section). Infantry parties work on this ~~by~~ in night & day shifts.	
			The Rly line (double track) running due N. from ALBERT was cut by this Coy in two places for a distance of 30ft. at the points Q 24 a 2 5 + Q 35 b 5 2 (Rly Map France sheet 57 D S.E) The work was completed on 14th inst. It is supposed that the Germans by some means were using this for communication purposes.	
"	25/3/16		Work on dug outs proceeds Inf Parties supplied by 11th R In Fus	
"	26/3/16		do do	
			Party also working on making beds in billets – another party on making new water troughs for MARTINSART.	
"	27/3/16		do do Inf. supplied by 10th R. In. Fus. Lt. Ryan left the Coy for duty with 91st Fd Coy R.E. 64162 L/Cpl Orr S. died of G.S.W. recd 18/3/16 B.E.F.	

T2134. Wt. W708–776. 500000. 4/15. Sir J. C. & S.

27

Army Form C. 2118.

Instructions regarding War Diaries and Intelligence Summaries are contained in F. S. Regs., Part II. and the Staff Manual respectively. Title pages will be prepared in manuscript.

WAR DIARY ~~or~~ of 121st. Field Coy R.E.
~~INTELLIGENCE~~ ~~SUMMARY~~.

(*Erase heading not required.*)

Place	Date	Hour	Summary of Events and Information	Remarks and references to Appendices
MARTINSART	28/3/16		Work on dug outs at GORDON CASTLE, PAISLEY AV. ELGIN AV. WADE LANE BROMIELAW ST. continues – also maintenance of JACOB'S LADDER by Lt Ferrier. Infantry Parties supplied by 10th R. Innis. Fus.	
			Work on new water troughs for MARTINSART continues. 3 carpenters are employed.	
			Lt. A. J. Fawcett was transferred from 4th Bridging Train to this unit & reported for duty today.	CC
"	29/3/16		do. do. Infantry Parties supplied by 10th R In. Fus. & 14th R. I. Rifles	CC
"	30/3/16		do do do Infantry Parties supplied by 10th R In. Fus & 14th R I Rifles	CC
"	31/3/16		do do do Infantry Parties supplied by 14th R. I. Rifles. The weather has been very fine for the past three days.	CC

C Craig Major, R.E.
O.C. 121st Field Coy., R.E.

T2134. Wt. W708–776. 500000. 4/15. Sir J. C. & S.

28

Instructions regarding War Diaries and Intelligence Summaries are contained in F. S. Regs., Part II. and the Staff Manual respectively. Title pages will be prepared in manuscript.

WAR DIARY or INTELLIGENCE SUMMARY.

(*Erase heading not required.*)

of 121st Field Coy. R.E.

Army Form C. 2118.

Place	Date	Hour	Summary of Events and Information	Remarks and references to Appendices
MARTINSART	1/4/16		The making of dug-outs for bomb-stores etc + men continues at GORDON CASTLE, PAISLEY AV	
			Repairs to WHITCHURCH ST. + JACOBS LADDER	
			Bombproofing well head MARTINSART.	
			Infantry supplied by 14th Royal Irish Rifles	CC
"	2/4/16		do do do	CC
			Infantry supplied by 9th Royal Inniskilling Fusiliers	
			Excavation of creeping Trench from WHITCHURCH ST. to GEORGE ST. at night - superintended by NCOs + Sapper.	CC
"	3/4/16		do do do.	CC
			Infantry supplied by. 9th R. Innis Fus.	
"	4/4/16		do do do	
			Infantry supplied by 9th + 11th R. Innis Fus.	CC
			do do do	
"	5/4/16		do do do	CC

T2134. Wt. W708–776. 500000. 4/15. Sir J. C. & S.

29

Instructions regarding War Diaries and Intelligence Summaries are contained in F. S. Regs., Part II. and the Staff Manual respectively. Title pages will be prepared in manuscript.

WAR DIARY of ~~INTELLIGENCE SUMMARY.~~

(Erase heading not required.)

121st Field Coy R.E.

Army Form C. 2118.

Place	Date	Hour	Summary of Events and Information	Remarks and references to Appendices
MARTINSART	6/4/16		Dugouts & Bomb stores GORDON CASTLE, Revetting & traversing WHITCHURCH St. & ELGIN AV. dugouts & Bomb stores ELGIN AV. Infantry Parties supplied by 11th R Innis. Fus.	C.C.
"	7/4/16		do do	C.C.
"	8/4/16		Infantry Parties supplied by 10th R Innis Fus.	C.C.
"	9/4/16		do do Infantry Parties supplied by 10th R Innis Fus. & 14th R.Ir. Rifles	C.C.
"	10/4/16		Working Parties rearranging & working as per attached schedule 'A' 82814 Sapper Adams V.E. died of Pneumonia	C.C. "A"
"	11/4/16		do do ↖ {57634 Sapper Melville R. died of wounds rec'd 5.4.16	C.C.
"	12/4/16		do do {Interred Local Cemetery BEAUVAL	C.C.
"	13/4/16		do do	C.C.
"	14/4/16		do do	C.C.
"	15/4/16		do do	C.C.
"	16/4/16		do do	C.C.
"	17/4/16		do do Lieut J.E. Stewart joined the Coy from 3rd Field Squadron R.E.	C.C.

T2134. Wt. W708—776. 500000. 4/15. Sir J. C. & S.

Instructions regarding War Diaries and Intelligence Summaries are contained in F. S. Regs., Part II. and the Staff Manual respectively. Title pages will be prepared in manuscript.

30

WAR DIARY
~~or~~
~~INTELLIGENCE SUMMARY.~~
(*Erase heading not required.*)

121st Field Coy R.E.

Army Form C. 2118.

Place	Date	Hour	Summary of Events and Information	Remarks and references to Appendices
MARTINSART	18/4/16		Work proceeds as for 17-4-16	CC
"	19/4/16		Working Parties are as on attached schedule B	
			57543 Sapper Walker A died of Cerebro Spinal Meningitis	CC
			Interred in Local Cemetery VILLERS-BOCAGE Grave marked H 53	
"	20/4/16		working parties as for 19-4-16	CC
"	21/4/16		working parties as per attached schedule C.	CC
"	22/4/16		do do (no night parties due to a prearranged raid by German trenches at R 31 a. 4. 2)	CC
"	23/4/16		(Easter Sunday) do do - day parties stopped worked 1 p.m. night parties as usual	CC
"	24/4/16		(Easter Monday) Holiday for day & night parties	CC
			Progress report for work done by this Coy for the month ending is attached & marked "D"	
"	25/4/16		work as in schedule D. very fine weather	CC
"	26/4/16		do do	CC
"	27/4/16		do do	CC
"	28/4/16		do do	CC
"	29/4/16		do do	CC

31.

Army Form C. 2118.

Instructions regarding War Diaries and Intelligence Summaries are contained in F. S. Regs., Part II. and the Staff Manual respectively. Title pages will be prepared in manuscript.

WAR DIARY or INTELLIGENCE SUMMARY. of 121st Field Coy. RE.

(*Erase heading not required.*)

Place	Date	Hour	Summary of Events and Information	Remarks and references to Appendices
MARTINSART	30/4/16	Sunday	Work as in Schedule "D" Weather very fine. Working parties cease work at 12.30 P.M.	CC

[signature] Major, R.E.
O.C. 121st Field Coy., R.E.
30-4-16.

2353 Wt. W2544/1454 700,000 5/15 D. D. & L. A.D.S.S. Forms/C 2118.

A

121 st. Field Coy. R.E.

Index Letter	Nature of Work	RENDEZVOUS	hour	no of working Party	R.E. Officer i/c	R.E. N.C.O. i/c	Infantry found by
B	Bomb stores Bde Depot PAISLEY AV	R.E. H.Q. MARTINSART	8 am.	20	Lt Fawcett	Cpl Jackson	12 th R. I. R.
C	Bde. H.Q. Pa	"	"	10	"	Sgt. Agnew	"
D	Dugouts for 1 Coy. PAISLEY AV	"	"	80	"	"	"
E	Seven Dugouts GORDON CASTLE	"	"	40	Lt. Wilson	Sgt. Wilson	"
G	Bde. H.Q. Railway View	MESNIL	"	20	Lt. Gooch	Sgt. Warry	9th R. Ir. Fus.
	"	"	7 pm.	25	"	"	"
H	Preserved Ration store	"	8 a.m.	30	"	"	"
I	Btn H.Q. HAMEL	"	"	"	"		
M	Divl Preserved Ration store.				Lt. Gooch		9 th R. Ir. Fus.
N	Heavy Trench M. B.	MESNIL	8 a.m.	60	Lt. Ferrier		"
O	Bde Grenade Store				Lt. Gooch		"
P	" Command Post HAMEL	"	"	30			

121st. Field Coy. R.E.

Index Letter	Nature of Work	Rendezvous	hour	no of working Party	Officer (RE) i/c	R.E. N.C.O. i/c	Infantry Battn. Supplying
Q	R.E. stores General Work	R.E. H.Q. MARTINSART	8 a.m.	12	-	C.S.M. Mew	12th R.I.R.
R.	R.E. Divisional Dump	"	8 a.m.	25	Report to Sergt. Ferguson at Divl. Dump.		
S.	R.E. Loading Party.	"	5.30 p.m.	10	Report to C.S.M. Mew 121st. Field Coy R.E.		

121st. Fd. Coy. R.E.

Working Parties required for 19th Apl. on

Index letter	Nature of work	Rendezvous	Hour	Number of working party	Officer i/c	N.C.O. i/c	Remarks.
B.	Bomb store (Brigade Depot) PAISLEY AVE.	R.E. H.Q.	8 am	20	Lieut. Fawcett	Cpl Jackson	12th R.I.R.
C.	Bde. H.Q. PAISLEY AVE.	"	"	35	"	Sgt Agnew	"
D.	Dugouts for 1 Coy ".	"		70	"	"	"
E.	7 Dug outs GORDON CASTLE.	"		35	" Wilson	Sgt Wilson	"
G.	Bde. H.Q. RAILWAY VIEW.	MESNIL.	"	20.	" Gooch.	Sgt Henry	9th R.I.F.
H.	Runners Dugout	"	"	30	" Gooch		"
I.	Batt. H.Q. HAMEL.						
J.	R.E. Store Carrying party.	"	7pm	15	" Price		"
K.	Shelter Trenches.	R.E. H.Q.	8 am.	25	C.S.M. Mew.		

Index Letter	Nature of work	Rendezvous	Hour	Number of Infantry working Party.	Officer i/c.	N.C.O. i/c	Remarks.
M.	Preserved Ration store Divl.				Lieut. Gooch		
N.	Heavy Trench M. B.	MESNIL.	8am	60			
O.	Bde. Grenade store.				Lieut. Ferrier.		
P.	Bde. Command Post HAMIL.	"	"	30	" Gooch.		
Q.	R.E. Stores General work.	R.E.H.Q.	"	12	C.S.M. New		
R.	R.E. Divisional Dump.		"	25	Report to Sgt Ferguson at Divl. Dump.		
S.	R.E. Loading Party.	"	5.30pm	10	Report to C.S.M. New 121st Coy R.E.		

121st Field Coy RE

Working Parties for

Index Letter	Nature of Work	Rendezvous	Hour	Hour of leaving work	No of working Parties	RE O/C	RE NCO i/c	Parties found by.
A	Bomb store PAISLEY AV.	R.E. H.Q. Martinsart	8 am	3 pm	20	Lt Fawcett	Sergt Agnew	11th R.I.R.
B	Bde H.Q. PAISLEY AV.	"	"	"	40	"	"	"
C.	JACOB'S LADDER	Rly. Station MESNIL	"	"	30	Lt Ferrier	–	"
E	Petrol store THIEPVAL WOOD	R.E. H.Q. Martinsart	"	"	10	Lt Wilson	Sgt Leathem	"
F	7 dug-outs BELFAST CITY	"	"	"	40	"	Sgt Wilson	"
G	Bde H.Q RAILWAY VIEW	Rly station MESNIL	"	"	25	Lt Grock	2nd Cpl McInnes	"
J	Orderly dugout HAMEL	"	"	"	25	"	L/Cpl. Rainbird	"
M	H.T.M Batty. HAMEL	"	"	"	60	Lt Ferrier		"
N	Slit Trench	R.E. H.Q. Martinsart	"	"	40	Lt Stewart	Sgt Gordon	"
O	R.E. General Store	"	"	"	12	"	CSM. Mew	"
P.	RE Loading Party	"	5.30 pm	11 pm	12	"	"	"
S	JACOB'S LADDER	Rly station MESNIL	7.30 pm	1 am	100	Lt Ferrier	–	"

"S" is work under Bde. arrangements. The remainder is Divl. work

121st. Field Coy. R.E.

Progress Report of Works ending 21st. Apl. 16 as requested in X Corps GM 59 dt. 10.4.16

A. No front line trench work has been done.

B. Repairs have been done to WHITCHURCH ST.

C. 1. Three shell-proof shelters for Bde H.Q. (No 1) at PAISLEY AV. have been 3/4 completed.

2. Four shell proof shelters for Bde. HQ No 2 at PAISLEY AV. have been 3/4 completed.

3. Seven shell proof shelters "BELFAST CITY" in THIEPVAL WOOD have been 7/8 completed.

4. Shell proof shelters for 1 Coy. at PAISLEY AV have been 1/4 completed.

5. One RAMC collecting station, elephant shell proof shelter at BLUFF N. of AUTHUILLE has been completed.

6. One advanced dressing station at GORDON CASTLE has been completed.

7. One Coy. H.Q. shell proof shelter in WHITCHURCH ST. has been completed.

8. A second entrance to BOMB STORE GORDON CASTLE was completed.

9. One shell proof shelter for bombers at GORDON CASTLE was 9/10 completed

C 10 Water tank at GORDON CASTLE was shell proofed.

11 Two shell proof shelters W. end of WAITCHURCH ST were completed.

12 Pump house at THIEPVAL WOOD was shell proofed

13 Engine & pump houses at MARTINSART were shell proofed

14 Battn H.Q HAMEL 45% completed

15 Two heavy Trench Mortar Emplacements and shelters at HAMEL 35% completed

16 One Coy. H.Q. shell proof shelter at HAMEL 85% completed.

17 Four dugouts Brigade H.Q on HAMEL ROAD $\frac{1}{10}$ completed by this Coy. These are $\frac{9}{10}$ completed.

18 One Orderlies shell-proof shelter at HAMEL 28% completed.

F (1) A creeping trench between GEORGE ST. and WHITCHURCH ST $\frac{1}{3}$ completed

(2) Traversing ELGIN AV. $\frac{1}{8}$ completed

G made & erected and laid water pipe to horse troughs MARTINSART.

121. FCRE

Army Form C. 2118.

Vol 8

32

Instructions regarding War Diaries and Intelligence Summaries are contained in F. S. Regs., Part II. and the Staff Manual respectively. Title pages will be prepared in manuscript.

WAR DIARY
of 121st Field Coy. R.E.
~~INTELLIGENCE SUMMARY.~~
(*Erase heading not required.*)

XXXVI

Place	Date	Hour	Summary of Events and Information	Remarks and references to Appendices
MARTINSART.	1.5.16		Work as in Schedule "A". Very fine weather.	CC
	2.5.16		do. do.	CC
	3.5.16		do. do.	CC
	4.5.16		do. do. The following men joined the Coy. from No. 4 General Base 57541 Sapr. Vaughan F. 64104 " Goode W. A. 64659 " Taggart R. G. 57703 Lce. Corpl. Dunwoody W. J. transferred to this Coy. from 150th Coy., permission of R.E. Records having been obtained. 64136 Dr. McIldoon D. joined Coy. from Base & transferred to 122nd. Field Coy. R.E.	CC
"	5.5.16		Working parties as in Schedule "A"	CC
"	6.5.16		do do	CC
"	7.5.16		do do	CC
"	8.5.16		do do	CC
"	9.5.16		do do	CC

T2134. Wt. W708—776. 500000. 4/15. Sir J. C. & S.

33

Army Form C. 2118.

Instructions regarding War Diaries and Intelligence Summaries are contained in F. S. Regs., Part II. and the Staff Manual respectively. Title pages will be prepared in manuscript.

WAR DIARY of 121st Field Coy R.E.

~~INTELLIGENCE~~ SUMMARY.

(*Erase heading not required.*)

Place	Date	Hour	Summary of Events and Information	Remarks and references to Appendices
MARTINSART	10/5/16		Working parties as in schedule "A"	CC
"	11/5/16		" "	CC
"	12/5/16		" "	CC
"			69663 Sapper Ryan T. wounded by shrapnel	
"	13/5/16		Working Parties as in schedule "A"	CC
"	14/5/16		do do	CC
"	15/5/16		do do	CC
"	16/5/16		do do	CC
"	17/5/16		do do	CC
			64010 Dr Start F, 64042 Dr McIlwaine R joined unit from Base.	CC
"	18/5/16		Working parties have been rearranged and now work as shown in Schedule "B"	CC
"	19/5/16		do do	CC
"	20/5/16		do do	CC
"	21/5/16		do do	CC
			The weather has been very warm for the past few days.	

T2134. Wt. W708—776. 500000. 4/15. Sir J. C. & S.

Instructions regarding War Diaries and Intelligence Summaries are contained in F. S. Regs., Part II. and the Staff Manual respectively. Title pages will be prepared in manuscript.

34

WAR DIARY of 121st. Field Coy. R.E.

~~INTELLIGENCE SUMMARY.~~

(Erase heading not required.)

Army Form C. 2118.

Place	Date	Hour	Summary of Events and Information	Remarks and references to Appendices
MARTINSART	22/5/16		Working Parties as in schedule "B"	
			The progress report of works done by the Coy from 21/5/16 to 22/5/16 is attached & marked "C"	
			This includes the work done by No 3 section under Lt. Ferrier at MESNIL. This section is working under 108th Infantry Brigade.	C.E.
"	23/5/16		Working Parties as in schedule "B"	
			64005 Sapper Malone J. was killed by M.G. Bullet on night of 23/24 while working on a new M.G. emplacement at Q17d03	C.E.
"	24/5/16		Working Parties as in schedule "B"	C.E.
"	25/5/16		As no working Parties are available today our men had a holiday & spent the day in bathing & general cleaning up. Pay Parade in the afternoon	C.E.
"	~~26/5/16~~			
"	26/5/16		Working parties as in schedule "B"	C.E.

35/

Instructions regarding War Diaries and Intelligence Summaries are contained in F. S. Regs., Part II. and the Staff Manual respectively. Title pages will be prepared in manuscript.

WAR DIARY or ~~INTELLIGENCE~~ SUMMARY.

(Erase heading not required.)

121st Field Coy R.E.

Army Form C. 2118.

Place	Date	Hour	Summary of Events and Information	Remarks and references to Appendices
MARTINSART	27/5/16		Working parties as in "B" Fine weather	CC
"	28/5/16		(Sunday) do Experiment with Bangalore torpedo for cutting barbed wire entanglement proved very successful	CC
"	29/5/16		Working parties as in "B" weather fine	CC
"	30/5/16		" "	CC
"	31/5/16		Nos. 1 + 2 sections moved this evg into dug outs at Q 29 b 5.8 Reference Map France 57D S.E. Edition 2a 122nd Field Coy R.E. (two sections) approximately move into the billets occupied by our two sections. The dugouts now occupied by our men were vacated by 150th Field Coy R.E. who have today gone back the line for a fortnights rest. Nos 1+2 sections are not on works today. Working parties shown in B have been supplied by 10th R.I.R. with the exception of 85 men from 15th R.I.R.	CC

C Craig Major
OC 121st Field Co RE
36th Division
31-5-16

T2134. Wt. W708—776. 500000. 4/15. Sir J. C. & S.

A

121ST. FIELD COMPANY. R.E.

WORKING PARTIES REQUIRED FOR APRIL 28TH. AND UNTIL FURTHER ORDERS?.

Index Letter.	NATURE OF WORK.	RENDEZVOUS.	HOUR.	HOUR OF LEAVING WORK.	NUMBER OF WORKING PARTIES.	OFFICER i/c.	N.C.O. i/c.	REMARKS.
A.	BOMB STORE. PAISLEY AVENUE.	MARTINSART. R.E., H.Q.	8 a.m.	3 p.m.	20	Lt. Fawcett.	Sergt. Agnew.	11th Royal Ir.Rifles. MARTINSART.
B.	BDE. H.QRS. PAISLEY AVENUE.	- do -	8 a.m.	3 p.m.	40	- do -	- do -	- do -
C.								
D.								
E.								
F.	7 DUG-OUTS. BELFAST CITY.	R.E., H.Q. MARTINSART.	8 a.m.	3 p.m.	40	- do -	Sergt. Wilson.	- do -
G.	BDE. H.QRS. RAILWAY VIEW.	RAILWAY STN. MESNIL.	8 a.m.	3 p.m.	25	Lt. Gooch.	2/cpl.M'Innis.	11th Royal Ir.Rifles. MESNIL.
H.								
O.	R.E. GENERAL STORE.	R.E.,H.Q. MARTINSART.	8 a.m.	3 p.m.	12	Lt. Stewart.	C.S.M.	11th Royal Ir.Rifles. MARTINSART.
P.	R.E. LOADING PARTY.	- do -	5-30 p.m.	11 p.m.	12	- do -	C.S.M.	- do -
N.	SLIT TRENCH.	- do -	8 a.m.	3 p.m.	80	- do -	Sergt. Gordon.	- do -
Q.	BDE. H. QRS. RAILWAY VIEW.	RAILWAY STN. MESNIL.	7 p.m.	1 a.m.	20	Lt. Gooch.	L/Cpl M'NEILL.	- do -
I.	BATT. H. QRS. HAMEL.(No 2).	- do -	8 a.m.	3 p.m.	30	- do -	L/Cpl M'Cooke.	- do -
J.	ORDERLY DUG-OUT - HAMEL.	- do -	8 a.m.	3 p.m.	25	- do -	L/Cpl Rainbird.	- do -
K.	BATTN.H. QRS. HAMEL.(No 3).	- do -	8 a.m.	3 p.m.	20	Lt. Wilson.		- do -
L.	BDE.RATION STORE. HAMEL.							
M.	H.T.M.BATTERY. HAMEL.	RAILWAY STN. MESNIL.	8 a.m.	3 p.m.	40	- do -		- do -

NOTE:- This table of working cancels all previous tables.

B

121st. Field Coy. R.E.

Working Parties required from 18.5.16 until further notice

Index Letter	Work	Men	Rendezvous	To report to	Hour	Finish work	R.E. N.C.O. i/c Party.
A	Flint Collecting Party	16	R.E. H.Q. MARTINSART	Lt. Fawcett D.	8 a.m.	3 p.m.	Sapper Leslie
C.	Petrol store Thiepval Wood	10	"	"	"	"	L.Cpl. Whelan.
D	Communication + assembly trenches Thiepval Wood.	250	"	"	"	"	Sgt Agnew.
E	Bde. H.Q. Railway View	15	"	Lt. Gooch	"	"	Cpl McNeill
F	Batt. H.Q. No 2 HAMEL	30	Rly. Station MESNIL	"	"	"	L.Cpl. McCooke
G	Orderlies dugout HAMEL	15	"	"	"	"	L.Cpl Rainbird
H	Obstacles MILL ROAD.	10	"	"	8 p.m.	2 a.m.	2nd Cpl McInness
I	4 T.M. Batt. Devial Av. HAMEL	45	R.E. H.Q. Martinsart	Lt. Wilson	8 a.m.	3 p.m.	Sergt. Gordon

Index Letter	Work	Men	Rendezvous	To report to	Hour	Finish Work	R.E. N.C.O. i/c Party.
J	Bathn. H.Q. No 3 HAMEL	25	R.E. H.Q. Martinsart	Lt. Wilson	8 a.m.	3 p.m.	Sgt. Wilson
K	Carrying Party	20	Rly station MESNIL	"	8 p.m.	2 a.m.	Sapper Adjey
L	R.E. General stores	12	R.E. H.Q. Martinsart	Lt. Stewart	8 a.m.	3 p.m.	C.S.M. Mew
M	R.E. Loading party	12	"	"	5.30 p.m.	11 p.m.	"
O	Regimental Aid post	10	"	Lt. Gooch	8 a.m.	3 p.m.	To be detailed
P	Water supply HAMEL	20	"	"	"	"	"
Q	Ration store HAMEL	10	"	"	"	"	"
R	Regimental Aid Post HAMEL	20	"	"	8 p.m.	2 a.m.	"

C/

121st Field Coy R.E.

Progress report of works ending 23rd May 1916 as requested in X Corps G.M. 59 dated 10. 4. '16.

Saps.

A. (1) Nos 14 + 15 have been extended to 100 yds in length and wired.

(2) New Fire trench Q 17 b to end of BUCKINGHAM PALACE RD. sap has been dug wired + 30% of firestep + parapet revetted

(3) Front line trench between BURREL AV. + BUCKINGHAM PALACE RD. has been deepened about 18" throughout.

B. 300 yds of old German trench between Q 23 b 0 9 & Q 17 C 5 3 has been deepened + at intervals the Firestep has been reversed.

C. 1 Three shell proof shelters for Bde H.Q. (No 1) at PAISLEY AV. have been completed

2 Four shell-proof shelters for Bde. H.Q. (No 2) at PAISLEY AV. have been completed.

6 (3) Seven shell proof shelters "BELFAST CITY" in THIEPVAL WOOD have been completed.

Two of the dugouts under (1) have been connected by a tunnel while the 3rd has a second entrance.

(4) Battalion H.Q. HAMEL has been 97% completed.

(5). Four dugouts Brigade H.Q. on HAMEL RD. have been 99% completed

(6) One orderlies shell proof shelter at HAMEL has been 93% completed

(7) One Coy. dug.out at JOFFRE AV. has been completed.

(8) Two shell proof shelters + No 1 H.T.M. emplacement at DEVIAL AV. HAMEL has been 75% completed.

(9) Two shell proof shelters + No 2 H.T.M emplacement has been 70% completed

(10) One Elephant shell proof shelter Battn. H.Q. HAMEL has been 54% completed

(11) One RAMC collecting station elephant shell proof shelter has been completed at PAISLEY AV.

(12) One existing RAMC elephant shel has been made shell proof

C(13). One R.A.M.C. elephant shelter has been lengthened 18'

These three dug-outs have been connected by a tunnel

(14) The structure of the pump house in THIEPVAL WOOD has been strengthened.

(15) A dug-out (shell-proof) 13'6"x8" has been 15% completed at GORDON CASTLE

(16) A shell proof shelter for a petrol store has been completed near pump house in THIEPVAL WOOD.

F.(1) A communication Trench 400 yds long 6' deep has been 85% completed at South end of SUTHERLAND AV.

(2) An evacuation Trench 6' deep from junction of PAISLEY AV & SUTHERLAND AV. to WHITCHURCH ST. has been 50% completed.

G(1) The strengthening of Regimental Aid post HAMEL has been 36% completed.

(2) The construction of ration store HAMEL has been completed.

(3) Water supply to Rly embankment at HAMEL has been completed.

G(4) Water supply Regimental Aid Post HAMEL has been 25% completed

K(1) Making main road in HAMEL suitable for wheeled traffic has been 75% completed.

(2) Brigade 2nd line has been deepened from JACOBS LADDER to front line.

G(4) Water supply Regimental Aid Post HAMEL has been 25% completed.
(5) RAMC dressing station MESNIL 5% under construction
(6) Slit trenches for this Coy in MARTINSART have been 95% completed
K(1) Trench from JACOB'S LADDER to MOUND KEEP - 10% deepened
(2) 50% JACOBS LADDER Trench floored, 10% revetted screening almost complete 250 yards deepened sump pits cleared
(3) Making main road in HAMEL suitable for wheeled traffic has been 75% completed.
(4) Brigade 2nd line has been deepened from JACOBS LADDER to front line.

C(continued) 17 dugout 18' x 8' SHORT ST. has been completed.

D(1) MG emplacement frame for THORNE AV. has been completed & handed over to 108th MG Coy:

(Sd) C Craig ...Major, R.E.
O.C. 121st Field Coy., R.E.

36th Divisional Engineers

121st. FIELD COMPANY R. E.

JUNE 1916

Instructions regarding War Diaries and Intelligence Summaries are contained in F. S. Regs., Part II. and the Staff Manual respectively. Title pages will be prepared in manuscript.

36

WAR DIARY or ~~INTELLIGENCE SUMMARY.~~

(*Erase heading not required.*)

of 121st Field Coy R.E.

XXVII

Army Form C. 2118.

Vol 9

Place	Date	Hour	Summary of Events and Information	Remarks and references to Appendices
MARTINSART	1.6.16		Owing to the relief of 108th Inf Bde by 147th Bde of 49th Divn no working parties were available today. Only Nos 1 + 2 sections were on Divl work No 3 section is still employed on Brigade Work. No 4 section was employed on fatigue work at CRE's 36 Divl Dump as Infantry had to move along with 108 Bde.	CC
"	2.6.16		Working parties are now found by 7th W Riding Regiment according to attached schedule A.	
			Lt Fawcett took charge of No 3 section in addition to his own (No 4) during Lt ~~Farrier's~~ absence on leave	
			The billets of the various sections now are H.Q. + No 4 MARTINSART No 3 MESNIL Nos 1 + 2 in dugouts at Q 29 b 5 5	CC
"	3.6.16		Working parties as in schedule A (Divisional Work) do B. (Brigade Work No 3 Section)	
			No night parties later than 12 p.m. (By order of 36 Div H.Q.)	CC

T2134. Wt. W708–776. 500000. 4/15. Sir J. C. & S.

37

Instructions regarding War Diaries and Intelligence Summaries are contained in F. S. Regs., Part II. and the Staff Manual respectively. Title pages will be prepared in manuscript.

WAR DIARY of 121st Field Coy. R.E.
or
~~INTELLIGENCE SUMMARY.~~
(*Erase heading not required.*)

Army Form C. 2118.

Place	Date	Hour	Summary of Events and Information	Remarks and references to Appendices
MARTINSART	4.6.16		(Sunday) Working parties as in schedule A (Divisional Work) do " B (Brigade Work) Parties left off work 1 pm. Health Inspection for H.Q. + No 4 sections.	
"	5/6/16		Working parties as for 4/6/16. No night parties On the night of 5/6th a raid was carried out by the 12th R.I.R. against the Railway Sap in the German lines in the HAMEL sector. Lieut Fawcett, 64636 Corpl McVicker J.H. 57505 Sapper Parkhill J. of this Coy. accompanied the party taking with them Bangalore Torpedoes and explosives with which they demolished the enemy's wire and blew up several dug outs. They also demolished the entrance to a tunnel running towards our lines. Sapper Parkhill also brought back valuable information regarding electric cables, trench tramways and R.E. material which he observed in the sap, tunnel + vicinity.	
"	6/6/16		Working parties as on 4/6/16	

T2134. Wt. W708—776. 500000. 4/15. Sir J. C. & S.

Instructions regarding War Diaries and Intelligence Summaries are contained in F. S. Regs., Part II. and the Staff Manual respectively. Title pages will be prepared in manuscript.

38

WAR DIARY of 121st Field Coy R.E. INTELLIGENCE SUMMARY.

(Erase heading not required.)

Army Form C. 2118.

Place	Date	Hour	Summary of Events and Information	Remarks and references to Appendices
MARTINSART	7/6/16		Working Parties for Divisional Work as in A. " Brigade " " B	CC
"	8/6/16		do do 57771 Corpl Anderson H. admitted Hospital (scabies)	CC
"	9/6/16		Working Parties as on 8th inst. 57446 Sapper Galway W. Admitted Field Ambce The raid mentioned on 5th inst. was the subject of 36 Divl Routine Order No 746. The organisation & execution of the enterprise was specially commended by the Divisional Commander	CC
"	10/6/16		Working Parties as on 9th inst 57653 Sapper McFadden D sent F.A. (Influenza)	CC
"	11/6/16		(Sunday) Work as on 10th - left off work 12 midday Health inspection in the afternoon Corpl Anderson discharged F.A.	CC
"	12/6/16		Work as on 11th. Lt. H.J. Palmer rejoined Coy. from 36th Divl School of Instruction & took command of No 3 section	CC
"	13/6/16		Working parties have been slightly changed. Those marked × have been left off by C.R.E. 36 Div. Orders Lt. Ferrier A. joined 36th Div School of Inst. on returning from leave (instead of Lt Palmer (joined Coy)	CC

39

Instructions regarding War Diaries and Intelligence Summaries are contained in F. S. Regs., Part II. and the Staff Manual respectively. Title pages will be prepared in manuscript.

WAR DIARY or ~~INTELLIGENCE SUMMARY.~~

(Erase heading not required.)

of 121st Field Coy R.E. 36th Divn

Army Form C. 2118.

Place	Date	Hour	Summary of Events and Information	Remarks and references to Appendices
MARTINSART	14/6/16		Working parties as in schedule A + B + 100 men have also been obtained for work as shown on "C" 57404 Sergt. Agnew S. wounded by shrapnel in wrist. Sapper Galway discharged from F.A. 13/6/16 103013 Sapper Reid J. admitted F.A. 12/6/16. The weather for the past week has been far from fine. There has been rain almost every day	
"	15/6/16		Parties as for 14th inst. Slit trenches are being prepared in MARTINSART for occupation by the Coy in case of bombardment.	
"	16/6/16		Working parties shown in A have been reduced + the men concentrated on B, E, J + L. – 75 men working on stretcher communication trench HAMEL. One section of 150th FIELD COY employed on gas curtaining dressing stations HAMEL. Cellars in MARTINSART were obtained for the men in case of a bombardment. — weather good	

2353 Wt. W2544/1454 700,000 5/15 D. D. & L. A.D.S.S./Forms/C. 2118.

40

Instructions regarding War Diaries and Intelligence Summaries are contained in F. S. Regs., Part II. and the Staff Manual respectively. Title pages will be prepared in manuscript.

WAR DIARY or ~~INTELLIGENCE SUMMARY~~. of 121st Field Coy. R.E.

(*Erase heading not required.*)

Army Form C. 2118.

Place	Date	Hour	Summary of Events and Information	Remarks and references to Appendices
MARTINSART.	17/6/16		Working parties are. H T M. Batty HAMEL 12 men Battn HQ do 44 men. Reg. Aid Post do 10 men McMahons Av 29 men PAISLEY AV. dugouts 25 men. Stretcher Communication trenches 150 men. One section of 130th. Fd Coy. R.E. ges-curtaining dressing-stations in HAMEL sector.	CC
"	18/6/16		do do Arrangements have been made for bivouacing transport of Coy at P36 b 90 when the prearranged bombardment takes place. Secret Instructions have already been issued on the subject. Transport of the 3 Fd Coys of 36th Divn bivouacs at same place. The tool carts of the 3 sections on detachment have been brought here this evg.	CC
"	19/6/16		Work as on 18th inst. Tool cart equipment being overhauled No 3 section in the evg. moved from MESNIL to cellars in MARTINSART	CC

41

Instructions regarding War Diaries and Intelligence Summaries are contained in F. S. Regs., Part II. and the Staff Manual respectively. Title pages will be prepared in manuscript.

WAR DIARY
or
~~INTELLIGENCE~~ ~~SUMMARY~~.

(Erase heading not required.)

121st Field Coy R.E.

Army Form C. 2118.

Place	Date	Hour	Summary of Events and Information	Remarks and references to Appendices
MARTINSART	20/6/16		Practically all the works in hand of this Coy have now been completed.	
			Nos. 1 + 2 sections, late in the evg. marched from their dugouts at COOKERS HAMEL to MARTINSART and were accommodated in billets there.	
			The following joined Coy from base	
			64489 Sapper McClung C.	
			64688 " Millar K.	
			64011 Driver Molyneux	
			57609 Sapper Hall A. and Transferred 150th Fd Coy R.E.	
			64253 LCpl. Geldea J. " 122nd "	
			64480 Sapper Martin J. } joined 150th Coy R.E. from Base	
			57426 " Campbell R } + as they formerly belonged to	
			57736 " Curry R } this Coy transferred to it	
			64454 " Johnston J } same day.	
			64047 Sapper Dixon J.W. wounded by shrapnel 19/6/16	
			57774 " McKnight W.J. do 16/6/16	

2353 Wt. W2544/1454 700,000 5/15 D. D. & L. A.D.S.S. Forms/C. 2118

42

Instructions regarding War Diaries and Intelligence Summaries are contained in F. S. Regs., Part II. and the Staff Manual respectively. Title pages will be prepared in manuscript.

WAR DIARY or ~~INTELLIGENCE~~ SUMMARY. of 121st Field Coy R.E.

(Erase heading not required.)

Army Form C. 2118.

Place	Date	Hour	Summary of Events and Information	Remarks and references to Appendices
MARTINSART	21/6/16		General arrangements for comforts of men ~~in~~ cellars	
			64403 Sapr Dockerty admitted Fd Amb.	
			57784 " Gamble J Transferred RETC Newark 9/6/16 (auth RE Records Chatham)	C.C.
"	22/6/16		H.T.M Battery emplacements being completed at HAMEL	
			Pontoons brought from FORCEVILLE & put in river ANCRE	C.C.
"	23/6/16		Transport moved into bivouac at Q36 b 80. This includes all mobilization equipment. Remaining stores are being put into store at 15 Rue de Mailly, there to be collected at a future date	C.C.
"	24/6/16		First day of bombardment which is by no means heavy. According to Secret Instructions this Coy is being held in reserve. One section is to be prepared to move with the ~~a~~ 107th Brigade. Stretcher trenches at HAMEL were marked Up and Down ~~to~~ ~~Torpedoes~~ Bangalore Torpedoes (Ammonal tubes) are being made. Also 300 Signalling Discs for 107, 108, & 109 Brigades	C.C.

2353 Wt. W2544/1454 700,000 5/15 D. D. & L. A.D.S.S. Forms/C. 2118.

43

Instructions regarding War Diaries and Intelligence Summaries are contained in F. S. Regs., Part II. and the Staff Manual respectively. Title pages will be prepared in manuscript.

WAR DIARY or ~~INTELLIGENCE SUMMARY~~. 121st Field Coy. R.E.

(Erase heading not required.)

Army Form C. 2118.

Place	Date	Hour	Summary of Events and Information	Remarks and references to Appendices
MARTINSART	25/6/16		V day - 2nd day of bombardment which has increased very considerably. Ammonal tubes still being made. Discs have been completed. Two large periscopes are being made for R.A. also an O.P. at Divisional Report centre. The section referred to on 24th inst is No 4 under Lieut Fawcett.	OC
"	26/6/16		W day - 3rd day of bombardment. The periscopes and O.P. have been completed today - work on ammonal tubes still continues. Two heavy bridges have been put across trenches between MESNIL and HAMEL.	OC
"	27/6/16		X day - 4th day of bombardment. Three small shells were dropped on E end of village in the morning. - work on Ammonal Tubes continues. On the night 27/28 several shells were dropped in village causing a few casualties - none in this Coy. Rations during the bombardment consist of bully beef, biscuit jam pea soup tea & sugar	OC

T2134. Wt. W708—776. 500000. 4/15. Sir J. C. & S.

44

Instructions regarding War Diaries and Intelligence Summaries are contained in F. S. Regs., Part II. and the Staff Manual respectively. Title pages will be prepared in manuscript.

WAR DIARY or ~~INTELLIGENCE SUMMARY~~. of 121st Field Coy R.E. 36th Divn

(*Erase heading not required.*)

Army Form C. 2118.

Place	Date	Hour	Summary of Events and Information	Remarks and references to Appendices
MARTINSART	28/6/16		Y day - 5th day of bombardment. Orders received from C.R.E. 36th Divn at 3pm. for Coy to be ready to move off at 7.30 a.m on 29/6/16 - day of assault. These orders were cancelled about 4.30pm as the day of assault has been postponed. Work continues on Bangalore torpedoes	OC
"	29/6/16		Originally the day for assault but now postponed. Dugout at Q31b 9.8 Reference 57D S.E 2b. being made for Divl R.E. H.Q. staff. Banggalore torpedoes still being made. Bombardment still continues. Several shells were dropped in village on night of 28/29. Comparatively little damage done with the exception of one shell which killed the majority of a platoon of 13th R.I.R. - no casualties as yet in this Coy.	OC
"	30/6/16		Bombardment continues - work on dugout + torpedoes continues. Trench ladders being made. A second O.P. for 36 Divl HQ has been constructed at Q 25a 2.5. Ref 57D S.E 2b.	OC

C Craig Major
OC 121st Field Co. R.E.
30-6-16.

T2134. Wt. W708—776. 500000. 4/15. Sir J. C. & S.

A

121st. Field Coy. R.E.

Working Parties to be supplied by 7th W. Riding Regt. from 2-6-16

Index Letter	Work	Men	Rendezvous	To report to	Hour (Start)	Finish	R.E. N.C.O. i/c Party
A	Flint collecting party	16	R.E. H.Q. MARTINSART	Lt. Fawcett	8am.	3pm.	Sapper Leslie
B.	Coy. dug out PAISLEY AV.	40	"	"	"	"	Corpl McRoberts
C.	General's dug-out do	6	"	"	"	"	"
D	Bomb proofing cellar MARTINSART	10	"	"	"	"	Sergt. Mandall
E	Battn H.Q. No 3 HAMEL	25	R.E. dump bottom end of Jacob's Ladder HAMEL	Lt. Wilson	8.45a	3pm.	Sgt. Wilson
F	Heavy T.M. Battery do	45	"	"	"	"	Sgt. Gordon
G	Bde H.Q. RAILYWAY VIEW ✗	10	Battn dump bottom end of JACOB'S LADDER	Lt. Gooch	"	"	Corpl. McNeill
H	Battn H.Q. HAMEL ✗	30	"	"	"	"	L/Cpl McCooke
I	" ✗	10	"	"	3pm.	9pm.	Sapper Hanna
J	Orderlies dug-out HAMEL	15	"	"	8.30a	3pm.	L/Cpl. Rainbird

A

121st. Field Coy. R. E.

Working parties to be supplied by 7th W. Riding Regt. from 2/6/16 until further notice

Index Letter	Nature of Work	Men	Rendezvous	To report to	Hour	Finish	R.E. N.C.O. i/c Party
K	Orderlies dug-out HAMEL	10	Battn dump bottom end of JACOBS LADDER	Lt Gooch	3pm	9pm	Sapper Burston
L	Reg. Aid. Post HAMEL	10	"	"	8.30pm	3pm	L/Cpl. Heaney
M	R.E. General stores MARTINSART	12	R.E. H.Q. MARTINSART	Captn Stewart	8am	3pm	C.S.M. Mew.
N	Carrying party	20	Cookers HAMEL RD	Lt. Wilson	8.45pm	2am	Sapper Gowdy
O	Carrying R.E. stores	10	Battn dump bottom of JACOBS LADDER	Lt. Gooch	9pm	2am	Sapper Hendry
P	Battn H.Q. HAMEL	10	"	"	"	"	" Corpl. McInnes
Q	R.E. Loading party	12	R.E. H.Q. MARTINSART	Captn Stewart	5.30 pm	11pm	C.S.M. Mew

Work Tables for 121st Field Coy. R.E. to be found by 10th R.I.R.
Commencing ~~1st~~ 2nd June

Index No	Strength Off	Strength Men	Work	Rendezvous	Hour	Remarks
1	1	30	New Trench	MESNIL ST Cross roads	8 am.	
2	1	30	do	do	8 pm.	
3	1	30	JACOB'S LADDER	do	8 am.	
4	1	30	OLD GERMAN TRENCH	do	8 am.	
5	1	30	ROYAL AVENUE	do	8 am.	
6	-	20	M.G. emplacements	do	8 pm.	
7	1	40	PROSPECT TRENCH	do	8 am.	
8	-	20	To dig out French Communication Trench under O.C. 108th Bde M.G. Coy.	MESNIL CHURCH	8 pm.	To meet Officer 108 M.G. Coy. at MESNIL CHURCH. Party to bring 12 shovels + 8 picks to be provided Regimentally

(Sd) Bde Major
108th Bde

6

Working Parties supplied by 14th Royal Irish Rifles for 121st Field Coy R.E. on 14/6/16 + onwards.

Index No	Work	No of men	Report at	Time		
				Report	Finish work	
1	RAMC trench HAMEL	30	R.E. HQ MARTINSART	8 am.	3 pm.	
2	Strengthening old Regimental Aid Post	25	"	"	"	
3	H.T.M.B. HAMEL	10	"	2 pm.	9 pm.	
4	Bde H.Q. No 3 HAMEL	10	"	"	"	
5	woodcutting	5	"	8 am	3 pm	
6	Strengthening dugouts PAISLEY AV.	20	"	"	"	

10. ROYAL ENGINEERS.

One section 121 Field Coy, R.E., under Lieut. Fawcett, will be attached to Brigade Headquarters.

This section will march in rear of the 8th Bn. Royal Irish Rifles from AVELUY WOOD and will proceed by the Southern Causeway to the rearcAssembly Trench vacated by the 15th Bn. R. Irish Rifles in THIEPVAL WOOD near Brigade H.Q.

When in position Lieut. Fawcett will report at Brigade Headquarters.

36th Divisional Engineers.

121st FIELD COMPANY R. E.

JULY 1916

45

Instructions regarding War Diaries and Intelligence Summaries are contained in F. S. Regs., Part II. and the Staff Manual respectively. Title pages will be prepared in manuscript.

WAR DIARY or ~~INTELLIGENCE SUMMARY~~. of 121st Field Coy. R.E.

(Erase heading not required.)

Army Form C. 2118.

36 Divy
Vol 10

Place	Date	Hour	Summary of Events and Information	Remarks and references to Appendices
MARTINSART	1/7/16		Bombardment continued to 7.30 am when attack began. No 4 section of this Coy under Lieut Fawcett R.E. was attached to 107 Bde and moved into shelters in THIEPVAL WOOD at 4 am. They were engaged during the attack in evacuating the wounded from THIEPVAL WOOD to LANCASHIRE DUMP. The remainder of the Coy less mounted portion moved to N.E. corner of AVELUY WOOD at 6.30 am and awaited orders. The Coy remained all night in bivouac in the wood. Weather fine	CC
AVELUY WOOD	2/7/16		(Sunday) Bombardment continues. At 9.30 am orders were received to occupy the rough shelters at MOUND KEEP Q 35b 5.3 Ref map FRANCE 57D SE. The 36th (Ulster) Division was withdrawn from the line + orders received that (a) This Coy was to remain in the line + be attached to 147 Bde 49th Divn which relieved the 36th Divn (b) No 4 section which was with 107 Bde was to be attached 122nd Fd Coy R.E. + go back to rest with it (c) No 4 section of 122nd Fd Coy R.E. to be attached to this Coy	CC

2353 Wt. W2544/1454 700,000 5/15 D. D. & L. A.D.S.S./Forms/C. 2118.

46

Instructions regarding War Diaries and Intelligence Summaries are contained in F. S. Regs., Part II. and the Staff Manual respectively. Title pages will be prepared in manuscript.

WAR DIARY or ~~INTELLIGENCE~~ SUMMARY.

of 1/21st Field Coy R.E.

(*Erase heading not required.*)

Army Form C. 2118.

Place	Date	Hour	Summary of Events and Information	Remarks and references to Appendices
MOUND KEEP Q 35 b 5.3 Ref France 57D S.E.	3/7/16		Bombardment continues. The Coy was called on to repair the HAMEL-AVELUY road, and banks of canal + ANCRE river which was leaking - weather fine	C.D.
"	4/7/16		Heavy bombardment continues. The Coy was employed day and night on repairs and drainage of trenches in THIEPVAL WOOD, and converting ROSS ST, MEERUT ST and part of CHATEAU ST and CAUSEWAY SIDE which were communication trenches into support fire trenches. These trenches had all been knocked in by shell fire and gave little cover for our men to work in. There was exceptionally heavy and continuous rain in the afternoon, which filled the lower end of SANDY ROW ELGIN AV. and PAISLEY AV. trenches. The water for some distance was six feet deep. An outlet was cut as deep as the swamp alongside would permit + about 3 ft of the water drained off. Pumps were used to remove the remainder. In part of MEERUT ST there were so many dead bodies in an advanced stage of decomposition that it was impossible to move them without their coming to pieces. It was necessary to dig a new trench round	

2353 Wt. W2544/1454 700,000 5/15 D. D. & L. A.D.S.S./Forms/C. 2118.

47

Instructions regarding War Diaries and Intelligence Summaries are contained in F. S. Regs., Part II. and the Staff Manual respectively. Title pages will be prepared in manuscript.

WAR DIARY
or
~~INTELLIGENCE SUMMARY~~.
(*Erase heading not required.*)

121st Field Coy RE.

Army Form C. 2118.

Place	Date	Hour	Summary of Events and Information	Remarks and references to Appendices
Contd	4/7/16		that part, + fill in the old trench with the bodies in it. The heavy rain flooded our shelters at MOUND KEEP causing several of them to collapse. 57430 Sapper Dalton W and 57541 Sapper Vaughan J proceeded to ROUEN to be "released" for munition works with Messrs Harland + Wolff Belfast.	CC
MOUND KEEP do.	5/7/16		At 2am a shell fell in one of our dugouts severely wounding 52926 RSM McW C and 64636 Corpl McVicker JH and killing 67915 LCpl Cox J and 64006 Sapper Wylie E. The two remaining sappers in the dug out escaped with shell shock. These were 57768 Sapper Morgan J and 57718 Pte Gillespie R. They were sent to hospital. RSM McW C died on the way to hospital and Corpl McVicker died shortly after admission. The shelters had been constantly shelled for the past two days. Work was carried on by day and night on the trenches mentioned on the 4th inst – weather fine.	CC
do	6/7/16		Heavy bombardment continues. Work was carried on in trenches named on 4th inst. Very heavy rain fell from 2pm to 7pm again filling the trenches and rendering work most difficult. 57490 LCpl McDermott R J. wounded by shrapnel. 64169 Sapper Wright J who had been slightly wounded 2nd inst, + remained at duty was admitted to hospital.	CC

2353 Wt. W2544/1454 700,000 5/15 D. D. & L. A.D.S.S./Forms/C. 2118.

48

Instructions regarding War Diaries and Intelligence Summaries are contained in F. S. Regs., Part II. and the Staff Manual respectively. Title pages will be prepared in manuscript.

WAR DIARY
or
~~INTELLIGENCE SUMMARY.~~

(Erase heading not required.)

of 121st Field Coy RE

Army Form C. 2118.

Place	Date	Hour	Summary of Events and Information	Remarks and references to Appendices
MOUND KEEP	7/7/16		Bombardment continues - The 147th Bde was relieved by the 148th Bde, & this Coy was attached to 148th Bde. Work was continued on trenches named on 4th inst. Around our shelters was being so heavily shelled that the Coy was ordered by CRE 49th Div to sleep in Cellars in MARTINSART. We moved there in the afternoon - weather moderately fine.	
MARTINSART	8/7/16		Bombardment continues & work carried on in trenches named on 4th inst. At 4 pm orders were received to rejoin our own Division (36th Ulster) which had moved back. On return of our Sappers from the trenches all was got ready & the Coy moved off at 8.45 pm for HARPONVILLE reaching there at 12.30 am. 9th inst.	
			57496 Sapper McLaughlin J received shell shock on 2nd inst & was admitted Hospital.	C.C.
			~~Our total casualties from 1st July - day of assault were O.R. Two killed - two died of wounds two wounded by shrapnel and Three suffering from shell shock~~	

49

Instructions regarding War Diaries and Intelligence Summaries are contained in F. S. Regs., Part II. and the Staff Manual respectively. Title pages will be prepared in manuscript.

WAR DIARY or ~~INTELLIGENCE SUMMARY~~. 121st Field Coy R.E.

(Erase heading not required.)

Army Form C. 2118.

Place	Date	Hour	Summary of Events and Information	Remarks and references to Appendices
HARPONVILLE	9/7/16		(Sunday) The Company rested, & received orders to march to BEAUVAL the following morning - weather fine	CC
"	10/7/16		Coy moved off for BEAUVAL at 6.30 am arriving there at 12.15 pm. Two busses accompanied us to carry the most tired men - weather fine.	CC
BEAUVAL	11/7/16		The Coy moved off at 6.15 am for LE MEILLARD arriving there at 11 am & remaining there till 8 pm when it proceeded to Railhead at AUXI-LE-CHATEAU arriving 10.30 pm. Entraining began at 11 pm & was completed at 1 am - weather fine	CC
	12/7/16		Train moved off at 2 am arriving THIENNES 6.15 am. The Coy detrained, breakfasted there and marched for CAMPAGNE at 8 am arriving there 11 am - weather fine	CC

2353 Wt. W2544/1454 700,000 5/15 D. D. & L. A.D.S.S./Forms/C. 2118.

59

Army Form C. 2118.

Instructions regarding War Diaries and Intelligence Summaries are contained in F. S. Regs., Part II. and the Staff Manual respectively. Title pages will be prepared in manuscript.

WAR DIARY
or
INTELLIGENCE SUMMARY.
(Erase heading not required.)

7 1/2 Field Coy R.E.

Place	Date	Hour	Summary of Events and Information	Remarks and references to Appendices
SERQUES	13/7/16		marched to SERQUES at 6 15 am arriving 11 30 am. weather fine	C.C.
"	14/7/16		Coy employed in overhauling checking + cleaning equipment – weather fine	C.C.
"	15/7/16		do do weather fine	C.C.
"	16/7/16		(Sunday). Church parade 2 30 pm. – Pay parade 12 noon weather fine	C.C.
"	17/7/16		Training – squad drill etc from 8 am. to 12 noon – rest for remainder of day weather rather dull 57796 Sr [illegible] admitted hospital – sick	C.C.
"	18/7/16		Squad drill Physical drill + Rifle exercises 8 am. – 12 noon rest for remainder of day Weather dull but good	C.C.

2353 Wt. W2544/1454 700,000 5/15 D. D. & L. A.D.S.S./Forms/C. 2118.

51

Instructions regarding War Diaries and Intelligence Summaries are contained in F. S. Regs., Part II. and the Staff Manual respectively. Title pages will be prepared in manuscript.

WAR DIARY or ~~INTELLIGENCE SUMMARY.~~ 121st Field Coy R.E.

(*Erase heading not required.*)

Army Form C. 2118.

Place	Date	Hour	Summary of Events and Information	Remarks and references to Appendices
SERQUES	19/7/16		Route march including map-reading 8 am - 12 noon - rest for remainder of day. weather fine.	
"	20/7/16		Preparation for move on following day	
"	21/7/16		Coy moved from SERQUES to LEDRINGHEM. Time of march 8 am. to 3 P.M.	
LEDRINGHEM	22/7/16		Coy moved from LEDRINGHEM to ST MARIE-CAPPEL Time of march 7.45 am to 12 noon.	
ST MARIE-CAPPEL	23/7/16		Coy marched from ST MARIE CAPPEL to STEENWERCK accompanying 107 Infantry Brigade. Time of March 7.45 am to 4 p.m. Following on orders received from C.R.E. 36th Divn two men were detailed to run an oil engine on the STEENWERCK - NEUVE EGLISE road about 100 yards south of No 14 milestone. Also 1 N.C.O. + two men were detailed to take over saw from 96 Coy R.E. Ledon	
			Seven reinforcements joined Coy. from Base.	

Instructions regarding War Diaries and Intelligence Summaries are contained in F. S. Regs., Part II. and the Staff Manual respectively. Title Pages will be prepared in manuscript.

5V

WAR DIARY or ~~INTELLIGENCE~~ SUMMARY of 121st Field Coy R.E.

(Erase heading not required.)

Army Form C. 2118

Place	Date	Hour	Summary of Events and Information	Remarks and references to Appendices
STEENWERCK	24/7/16		General arrangement & cleaning up of new billets - weather dull. Fourteen reinforcements joined Coy from Base	CC
"	25/7/16		General work in billets. In afternoon bathing parades for all the Coy.	CC
"	26/7/16		Orders received from C.R.E. 36th Divn for Coy to move to camp 1 mile N. of LA CLYTTE on 27/7/16. This was cancelled later in the day. Men on detachment working engines at Baths on NEUVE EGLISE road joined Coy.	CC
"	28/7/16		Squad drill & Rifle exercises 9 am - 12 noon. - weather warm	CC
"	29/7/16		Coy moved to LE ROMARIN (France 36 N W. B 4 a 9 3) Billets which are small huts were taken over from 233 Coy R.E. 41st Division.	CC
ROMARIN	30/7/16		Improvement of Billets. Squad drill & rifle exercise. Pay Parade in afternoon - very warm weather. Officers reconnoitring Hill 63	CC

1875 Wt. W593/826 1,000,000 4/15 J.B.C. & A. A.D.S.S./Forms/C. 2118.

53

Instructions regarding War Diaries and Intelligence Summaries are contained in F. S. Regs., Part II. and the Staff Manual respectively. Title pages will be prepared in manuscript.

WAR DIARY of 121st Field Coy R.E.
or
~~INTELLIGENCE~~ SUMMARY.
(Erase heading not required.)

Army Form C. 2118.

Place	Date	Hour	Summary of Events and Information	Remarks and references to Appendices
ROMARIN B4a84 FRANCE 36 N.W.	31/7/16		Drawing R.E. stores – General improvement of billets Squad drill & rifle exercises – weather continues very hot. Officers reconnoitring Hill 63.	

C. Craig
Major, R.E.
O.C. 121st Field Coy, R.E.

54

Instructions regarding War Diaries and Intelligence Summaries are contained in F. S. Regs., Part II. and the Staff Manual respectively. Title pages will be prepared in manuscript.

WAR DIARY
or
~~INTELLIGENCE SUMMARY.~~
(*Erase heading not required.*)

121st Field Coy R.E.

Army Form C. 2118.

Vol 11

Place	Date	Hour	Summary of Events and Information	Remarks and references to Appendices
ROMARIN Ref France 36 N.W. B4a84	1/8/16		Repairs to Billets horse lines & general sanitary improvements. Trench work:- Communication & support trenches being deepened & repaired at U 13 d 3.7.	CC
	2/8/16		Repairs to billets etc as on 1st. Trench work as on 1st. Two coys. of No 8 Entrenching Battn were employed as working parties. Mined dugout at U 13 b 1 7 started	CC
"	3/8/16		Repairs to horse lines - drainage of foul drain. Trench work as on 2nd. Joiners working on frames for shelters. Trench work also includes repairs to FORT CLISSOLD and FORT EBERLE - 18 Reinforcements inoculated. Working parties from 8th Entrenching Battn amount to 400 men.	
"	4/8		Work as on 3rd. - 10% of Coy inoculated. This necessitates 48 hours off duty for each man inoculated.	CC
"	5/8/16		Trench work as above. Alterations to Divisional Baths on NEUVE EGLISE RD being carried out by No 3 section under Lieut Palmer. Shelter frames being made by joiners	CC

T2134. Wt. W708—776. 500000. 4/15. Sir J. C. & S.

55

Instructions regarding War Diaries and Intelligence Summaries are contained in F. S. Regs., Part II. and the Staff Manual respectively. Title pages will be prepared in manuscript.

WAR DIARY
or
~~INTELLIGENCE~~ SUMMARY.
(*Erase heading not required.*)

of 121st Field Coy R.E.

Army Form C. 2118.

Place	Date	Hour	Summary of Events and Information	Remarks and references to Appendices
ROMARIN	6/8/16		(Sunday) Kit & health inspection - no work - No 4 section under Lieut Fawcett moved into billets at T3 central (KENNEBAK.) for work under 107th Infantry Brigade	
"	7/8/16		Shelter frames being made - alterations to baths as on 5th inst. Trench work as on 5th inst. No working parties from No 8 Entrenching Battn. CC	
"	8/8/16		No 1 section under Lieut Gooch is detailed for work with O.C. 2nd Field Squadron R.E. This leaves No 2 section with remainder of No 3 section not working on baths available for Coy work. CC	
"	9/8/16		Joiners working on shelter frames. Trench work - dugouts in Subsidiary line O.Ps in HEATH trench and GAS trench - Working parties supplied by Cavalry. Avst 100 Work on Divl Baths Continues. CC	
"	10/8/16		Work as on 9th inst. - Weather which has been very warm since 1st rather cooler today CC.	

2353 Wt. W2544/1454 700,000 5/15 D. D. & L. A.D.S.S./Forms/C. 2118.

Instructions regarding War Diaries and Intelligence Summaries are contained in F. S. Regs., Part II. and the Staff Manual respectively. Title pages will be prepared in manuscript.

56

WAR DIARY or INTELLIGENCE SUMMARY.

(Erase heading not required.)

7 121st Field Coy R.E.

Army Form C. 2118.

Place	Date	Hour	Summary of Events and Information	Remarks and references to Appendices
ROMARIN	11/8/16		Joiners working on Trench frames. No 3 section - work on Divisional Baths No 2 " - Trench work - dugouts in SUBSIDIARY LINE and HEATH trench. O.Ps in HEATH trench and GAS trench. This work is done at night. Working parties found by Cavalry	C.C.
"	12/8/16		ditto	
"	13/8/16		(Sunday) Kit & health inspections - Payparade - no work Church Parades - Presbyterian 10 a.m. Church of Ireland 10.30 a.m.	C.C.
"	14/8/16		Work as on 11th inst	C.C.
"	15/8/16		work as on 11th inst - several heavy showers during the day. Two reinforcements joined Coy. 14th inst.	C.C.
"	16/8/16		work as on 11th inst.	C.C.

2353 Wt. W2544/1454 700,000 5/15 D. D. & L. A.D.S.S./Forms/C. 2118.

56

Instructions regarding War Diaries and Intelligence Summaries are contained in F. S. Regs., Part II. and the Staff Manual respectively. Title pages will be prepared in manuscript.

WAR DIARY of 121st Field Coy R.E.
or
~~INTELLIGENCE SUMMARY.~~
(Erase heading not required.)

Army Form C. 2118.

Place	Date	Hour	Summary of Events and Information	Remarks and references to Appendices
ROMARIN	17/8/16		No 4 section on detachment working with 107 Inf. Brigade No 1 " " " 2nd Field Squadron Part of No 3 section alteration to Baths on NEUVE EGLISE rd. No 2 + remainder of No 3 on Trench work viz Shelters of Subsidiary line. Also ablution benches at RED LODGE being installed. Joiners making Shelter frames Transport drawing Trench stores for use in Trenches	CC
"	18/8/16		as on 17th inst.	CC
"	19/8/16		as on 17th inst. working parties for Divisional work done by No 2 + 3 sections are supplied by Cavalry	CC
"	20/8/16		(Sunday) Church parades - Health kit + Gas helmet inspection no work	
"	21/8/16		as on 17th inst - Plumbers making Bangalore torpedoes	
"	22/8/16		as on 21st inst.	CC

2353 Wt. W2544/1454 700,000 5/15 D. D. & L. A.D.S.S./Forms/C. 2118.

57

Instructions regarding War Diaries and Intelligence Summaries are contained in F. S. Regs., Part II. and the Staff Manual respectively. Title pages will be prepared in manuscript.

WAR DIARY
or
~~INTELLIGENCE~~ SUMMARY. of 121st Field Coy. RE

(Erase heading not required.)

Army Form C. 2118.

Place	Date	Hour	Summary of Events and Information	Remarks and references to Appendices
ROMARIN	23/8/16		Work proceeds in making shelters off SUBSIDIARY LINE at LE ROSSIGNOL behind MACS RUIN H.T.M emplacement concrete being made at N36 d 5 4 Sheet 28 S W ~~France~~ Construction of 2 O Ps at U 13 b 3½ 2 and U 13 a 8 1 Sheet 28 S W France Alterations to Divisional Baths on NEUVE EGLISE road being carried out by part of No 3 section under Lieut Palmer Working parties found by Cavalry Weekly progress attached. Bangalore torpedoes being made by plumbers. Shelter frames by joiners. Transport drawing RE stores from DE SEULE for use in trenches.	CC
"	24/8/16		as on 23rd inst	CC
"	25/8/16		do do	CC
"	26/8/16		do do	CC
"	27/8/16		(Sunday) no works - Church parades - gas helmet inspection & pay parade	CC

58

Instructions regarding War Diaries and Intelligence Summaries are contained in F. S. Regs., Part II. and the Staff Manual respectively. Title pages will be prepared in manuscript.

WAR DIARY or ~~INTELLIGENCE SUMMARY.~~ of 121st Field Coy R.E.

(*Erase heading not required.*)

Army Form C. 2118.

Place	Date	Hour	Summary of Events and Information	Remarks and references to Appendices
ROMARIN	28/8/16		Work proceeds on shelters of SUBSIDIARY LINE at LE ROSSIGNOL behind Mac's Ruin. This work is done by night	
			H.T.M. Concrete emplacement being made at N 36 D 5 4	Sheet 28 S W France
			Construction of O.P's at U 13 b 3½ 2 and U 13 a 8 1	"
			Plumbers working on Bangalore Torpedoes.	
			Joiners making Trench frames.	
			Alterations to Divisional baths – No 3 section.	
			Transport drawing R.E. stores for Coys use	
			Three reinforcements joined Coy today. CC	
	29/8/16		Work as on 28th. No night parties owing to heavy rain. Party of six proceeded by motor lorry to DUNKERQUE for Boiler for Divisional Baths. CC	
"	30/8/16		Work as on 28th. Heavy rain in afternoon – no night parties. Party unloading boiler at Div^l Baths. CC	
"	31/8/16		Work as on 28th. – Weather has improved. Eight evacuations to C.C.S. took place in Coy during the month. Eight reinforcements joined Coy during month. CC	

C. Craig Major, R.E.
O.C. 121st Field Coy., R.E.

2353 Wt. W2544/1454 700,000 5/15 D. D. & L. A.D.S.S./Forms/C. 2118.

Weekly Progress Report of 121st Field Coy. R.E. 23/8/16

	Name or Map Ref.	Nature of work	Decimal of completion
Dugouts or shelters	Leading of Subsidiary line at Hr ROSSIGNOL behind MACs RUIN	Six shelters + trench leading to each completed One site for shelter excavated 3 excavations for 18' elephant dug outs completed 74 yards of trench leading to above excavated.	.1 .4
Divisional Baths	NEUVE EGLISE Road	alterations + extensions	.3
T.M. positions	N36 d 5 4	H.T.M. emplacement to be made of elephant + concrete 130 yards of Trench leading to emplacement dug 5' deep (old site was abandoned as there was too much water in it + land slides)	.1
O.P.s	U 13 b 3½ 2 U 13 a 8 1	Concrete structure	.2
Screening	U 13 a 8 8	Screen across road	1.
RAMC dressing station	PONT de St QUENTIN	one elephant sand bagged	.1

59

Instructions regarding War Diaries and Intelligence Summaries are contained in F. S. Regs., Part II. and the Staff Manual respectively. Title pages will be prepared in manuscript.

WAR DIARY
or
~~INTELLIGENCE SUMMARY.~~

(Erase heading not required.)

of 121st Field Coy R.E.

Army Form C. 2118.

Vol 12

Place	Date	Hour	Summary of Events and Information	Remarks and references to Appendices
LE ROMARIN	1.9.16		Trench Work Shelters being made in SUBSIDIARY LINE O.P.s in Heath trench + Gas trench. Working parties found by Cavalry. Divisional Bath. NEUVE EGLISE Rd. Repairs + alterations to – being carried out by part of No 3 section under Lieut Palmer. Carpenters shop Shelter frames being made. Transport drawing R.E. trench stores from DE SEULE dump to the different works.	[initials] [initials]
"	2.9.16		work as on 1st inst.	
"	3.9.16		(Sunday) – no work. Church parades. – health + Gas helmet Inspection – harness inspection.	[initials]

2353 Wt. W2544/1454 700,000 5/15 D. D. & L. A.D.S.S./Forms/C. 2118.

60

Instructions regarding War Diaries and Intelligence Summaries are contained in F. S. Regs., Part II. and the Staff Manual respectively. Title pages will be prepared in manuscript.

WAR DIARY or ~~INTELLIGENCE SUMMARY~~.

(*Erase heading not required.*)

of 121st Field Coy R.E.

Army Form C. 2118.

Place	Date	Hour	Summary of Events and Information	Remarks and references to Appendices
LE ROMARIN	4/9/16		Trench Work Shelters being made in Subsidiary Line O.P.'s in Heath Trench + Gas Trench H. T. M. emplacement (elephant + concrete) at N36D5'4 France 28 S.W. RAMC dressing stations at PONT de ST QUENTIN + ST QUENTIN CAB Working parties found by 8 Entrenching Battn. Divisional Baths NEUVE EGLISE road Repairs + alterations being carried out by part of No 3 section Carpenters shop. Shelter frames being made. Transport. drawing R.E. stores for use in trenches.	JS8
	5/9/16		as on 4th inst	JS8
	6/9/16		as on 4th inst.	JS8
	7/9/16		Collecting tools + packing up prior to moving No 1 + 2 sections moved in the evg to KENNEBAK	JS8
	8/9/16		HQ + No 3 sections with transport moved to ALDERSHOT CAMP.	JS8

2353 Wt. W2544/1454 700,000 5/15 D. D. & L. A.D.S.S./Forms/C. 2118.

61

Instructions regarding War Diaries and Intelligence Summaries are contained in F. S. Regs., Part II. and the Staff Manual respectively. Title pages will be prepared in manuscript.

WAR DIARY or ~~INTELLIGENCE SUMMARY~~ of 121st Field Coy R.E.

(Erase heading not required.)

Army Form C. 2118.

Place	Date	Hour	Summary of Events and Information	Remarks and references to Appendices
ALDERSHOT CAMP.	9/9/16		Part of No 3 section working on Improvements to Div^t Baths NEUVE EGLISE DE SEULE road	
			Remainder + HQ improving billets generally and drawing RE Stores from DE SEULE for use of sections in 107th Bde area.	BJS
DE KENNEBAK.			No 1 section (Lieut Gooch)	
			Repairs to SPRING WALK and DAY STREET } working parties	
			" to Billets at DE KENNEBAK } from 8th Ent. Batt^n	
			No 2 section (Lieut Wilson)	
			H.T.M. emplacement + Collecting Post RAMC – working parties by V_{36} T.M. + 16th R.I.R. (P.)	
			No 4 section (Lieut Fawcett) – on 107 Brigade work.	
			MG emplacement. Repairs to Agnes St. – Two 5.9 proof dugouts SURREY LANE. Working parties supplied by Battalions in reserve.	
	10/9/16		(Sunday) ~~no~~ work ~~all~~ Health + kit inspections	BJS.
	11/9/16		as on 9th	
	12/9/16		as on 9th	

2353 Wt. W2544/1454 700,000 5/15 D. D. & L. A.D.S.S./Forms/C. 2118.

62

Instructions regarding War Diaries and Intelligence Summaries are contained in F. S. Regs., Part II. and the Staff Manual respectively. Title pages will be prepared in manuscript.

WAR DIARY
or
INTELLIGENCE SUMMARY.
(Erase heading not required.)

Army Form C. 2118.

1210th Field Coy R.E.

Place	Date	Hour	Summary of Events and Information	Remarks and references to Appendices
ALDERSHOT CAMP	13/9/16		Capt J. E. Stewart took over Command of this Coy from Major Craig who is appointed O.C. Railhead Defences Second Army. Horse standings are being laid down here. Work proceeds as on 9th inst.	J.E.S.
	14/9/16		work as on 9th inst.	J.E.S.
"	15/9/16		" " 9th "	J.E.S.
"	16/9/16		" " "	J.E.S.
"	17/9/16		(Sunday) work proceeds as usual	
"	18/9/16		Trench work as on 9th. Horse standings & repairs to billets at Aldershot Camp. Divt Baths extension & erection of boiler - Neuve Eglise road.	J.E.S.
"	19/9/16		Work as on 18th inst.	
"	20/9/16		do. No work on night of 19th/20th. There has been considerable rain for the past few days which interfered with work on hand.	J.E.S.

2353 Wt. W2544/1454 700,000 5/15 D. D. & L. A.D.S.S./Forms/C. 2118.

63

Instructions regarding War Diaries and Intelligence Summaries are contained in F. S. Regs., Part II. and the Staff Manual respectively. Title pages will be prepared in manuscript.

WAR DIARY or ~~INTELLIGENCE SUMMARY~~. of 121st Field Coy R.E.

(Erase heading not required.)

Army Form C. 2118.

September 16

Place	Date	Hour	Summary of Events and Information	Remarks and references to Appendices
Aldershot Camp	21/9/16		Trench Work now is: Divl Work Cleaning river DOUVE + STUIVERBEEK (drainage of 70) Bde area Revetting Trenches – Day St Northumberland Av. + Medicine Hat Trail construction of M.G. emplacement no 2 Dugouts at Bays C2, C3 + D4 (Brigade Work under Lieut Fawcett) T.M. positions near Spring Walk + at N36C64½ (sheet 28) Collecting Post + Reg. Aid Post + Dressing station at Pont St Quentin St Quentin Cabt + Kandahar Farm Drying room for socks St. Quentin Cabt. Drying room for Gum boots T11a09½ Divl Baths Neuve Eglise Rd – Extension + erection of boiler. Horse standings Aldershot Camp. Transport drawing R.E. stores for trench work + material for construction of horse standings	
"	22/9/16		Work as on 21st. – weather wet.	GSS
"	23/9/16		do	
"	24/9/16		(Sunday). do in forenoon – In afternoon fitting Box Respirators	GSS

2353 Wt. W2544/1454 700,000 5/15 D. D. & L. A.D.S.S. Forms/C. 2118.

64

Instructions regarding War Diaries and Intelligence Summaries are contained in F. S. Regs., Part II. and the Staff Manual respectively. Title pages will be prepared in manuscript.

WAR DIARY or ~~INTELLIGENCE~~ SUMMARY.

of 121st Field Coy R.E.

(Erase heading not required.)

Army Form C. 2118.

September 1916

Place	Date	Hour	Summary of Events and Information	Remarks and references to Appendices
Aldershot Camp.	25/9/16		Work proceeds as on 21st inst.	S.E.S.
	26/9/16		do	S.E.S.
	27/9/16		do	S.E.S.
	28/9/16		do – no trench work before 11am. owing to prearranged bombardment. Weather has improved very much during the past four days.	S.E.S.
	29/9/16		work as on 21st inst	S.E.S.
	30/9/16		do	
			During the month we have had. Hospital admission – 13 Discharges – 4 Evacuations – 1 Reinforcements – 1	S.E.S.

S.E. Stewart Capt. R.E.
OC. 121st Field Coy R.E.

2353 Wt. W2544/1454 700,000 5/15 D. D. & L. A.D.S.S. Forms/C 2118.

65

Instructions regarding War Diaries and Intelligence Summaries are contained in F. S. Regs., Part II. and the Staff Manual respectively. Title pages will be prepared in manuscript.

WAR DIARY or ~~INTELLIGENCE SUMMARY~~.

(Erase heading not required.)

121st Field Coy R.E.

Army Form C. 2118.

Vol 13

October 1916

Place	Date	Hour	Summary of Events and Information	Remarks and references to Appendices
Aldershot Camp T19b63 (Sheet 28 S.W)	1/10/16		H.Q. + No 3 sections billeted here. Work: Extension to Divl Baths Neuve Eglise - De Seule Rd. ~~Repairs~~ Construction of horse standings in Camp here. Drawing R.E. Stores for use in Trenches.	J.E.S
Kennebak T3b 2 2 do	"		Nos 1 2 + 4 sections billeted here + working on Trench work Work: Drainage of 107 Bde area viz cleaning river Douve + Stinnebeek revetting + repairs to Trenches DAY ST SPRINGWALK NORTHUMBERLAND AV Construction of M G emplacement Elephant shelters at MACBRIDES MANSIONS FORBES Terr Dressing stations at ST QUENTIN + KANDAHAR FARM Drying rooms for socks + Gum boots at ST QUENTIN CABt and T 11 a 0 9½ (Sheet 28 S.W.) T. M. positions near SPRINGWALK and at N36C64½ Dugouts + shelters in front line - 107 Bde area under Lieut Fawcett. R.E.	J.E.S

T2134. Wt. W708—776. 500000. 4/15. Sir J. C. & S.

66

Instructions regarding War Diaries and Intelligence Summaries are contained in F. S. Regs., Part II. and the Staff Manual respectively. Title pages will be prepared in manuscript.

WAR DIARY
or
~~INTELLIGENCE SUMMARY~~.
(*Erase heading not required.*)

of 121st Field Coy R.E.

October 1916

Army Form C. 2118.

Place	Date	Hour	Summary of Events and Information	Remarks and references to Appendices
Aldershot Camp and De Kennebak	2/10/16		Work proceeds as on 1st inst.	S.E.S.
"	3/10/16		do do	S.E.S.
"	4/10/16		do - one man admitted F.A today very heavy rain.	S.E.S.
"	5/10/16		No work. The Coy. had a days "outing" to BAILLEUL under Div^l arrangements. Tea was provided - There was a Concert & cinema entertainment.	
"	6/10/16		Work proceeds as on 1st inst - weather improving	S.E.S.
"	7/10/16		Work as on 1st inst.	S.E.S.
"	8/10/16	(Sunday)	Work as on 1st inst. - Pay parade in the evg. Two men admitted F.A. sick.	S.E.S.
"	9/10/16		Work as on 1st. - One man discharged hospital	S.E.S.
"	10/10/16		do - Two reinforcements joined Coy from base	S.E.S.

Instructions regarding War Diaries and Intelligence Summaries are contained in F. S. Regs., Part II. and the Staff Manual respectively. Title pages will be prepared in manuscript.

67

WAR DIARY or ~~INTELLIGENCE SUMMARY.~~

(*Erase heading not required.*)

of 121st Field Coy RE

October 1916

Army Form C. 2118.

Place	Date	Hour	Summary of Events and Information	Remarks and references to Appendices
Aldershot Camp	11/10/16		Work proceeds as on 1st inst. – One man discharged from hospital.	SES
and De Kennebak	12/10/16		Work as on 1st inst. – but no working parties owing to reliefs of Battalions. A raid was carried out on the night of 11th/12th. on Divl front. Four sappers of this Coy took part in the raid with 107 Bde. & were very highly complimented for their work by O.C. 9th R.I.R.	SES
"	13/10/16		Work proceeds as on 1st inst.	SES
"	14/10/16		Trench work proceeds as on 1st Aldershot Camp – Horse standings and road leading into camp. Extension of hut – Transport drawing stores for trenches	SES
"	15/10/16		(Sunday) Work as on 14th inst.	SES
"	16/10/16		Work as on 14th inst – Bathing parade 4-5 pm	SES
"	17/10/16		Work as on 14th inst Four reinforcements joined Coy from Base	SES

T2134. Wt. W708–776. 500000. 4/15. Sir J. C. & S.

68

Instructions regarding War Diaries and Intelligence Summaries are contained in F. S. Regs., Part II. and the Staff Manual respectively. Title pages will be prepared in manuscript.

WAR DIARY
or
~~INTELLIGENCE SUMMARY.~~
(Erase heading not required.)

of 1210th Field Coy RE.

Army Form C. 2118.

October 1916

Place	Date	Hour	Summary of Events and Information	Remarks and references to Appendices
Aldershot Camp & De Kennebak	18/10/16		Trench work as on 1st inst.	[illegible]
			Work at Aldershot Camp	[illegible]
			Completion of Horse standings	
			Construction of road into Camp.	
			Transport drawing R.E. stores for Trench use	
	19/10/16		work as on 18th inst.	[illegible]
	20/10/16		do do	[illegible]
	21/10/16		do do	[illegible]
	22/10/16		(Sunday) do do – Pay Parade	[illegible]
"	23/10/16		Work as on 18th inst. – no working parties owing to relief	[illegible]
"	24/10/16		No work – "Outing" to Bailleul – wet afternoon	[illegible]
"	25/10/16		work as on 18th inst – weather wet.	[illegible]
"	26/10/16		do	[illegible]
"	27/10/16		do	[illegible]
"	28/10/16		do showery weather.	[illegible]
			one man admitted Field ambulance	[illegible]

T2134. Wt. W708–776. 500000. 4/15. Sir J. C. & S.

69

Instructions regarding War Diaries and Intelligence Summaries are contained in F. S. Regs., Part II. and the Staff Manual respectively. Title pages will be prepared in manuscript.

WAR DIARY of 121st Field Coy R.E.
or
~~INTELLIGENCE SUMMARY.~~
(Erase heading not required.)

Army Form C. 2118.

October 1916

Place	Date	Hour	Summary of Events and Information	Remarks and references to Appendices
Aldershot Camp + De Kennebak	29/10/16		Trench work as on 1st inst. Work at Aldershot Camp Construction of road leading to Camp Drainage of Camp.	S.F.S.
"	30/10/16		do do 57607 Sapper Gowdy W. J. awarded Military Medal by IX Corps Commander for distinguished conduct on a raid on German trenches on night 11th/12th inst.	S.F.S.
"	31/10/16		work as on 30th inst Eleven sappers of this Coy took part in a raid on German trenches on night 30th/31st Two men discharged from hospital	S.F.S.

R. Stewart Capt. R.E.
O.C. 121st Field Coy, R.E.

T2134. Wt. W708—776. 500000. 4/15. Sir J. C. & S.

69

Secret

Instructions regarding War Diaries and Intelligence Summaries are contained in F. S. Regs., Part II. and the Staff Manual respectively. Title pages will be prepared in manuscript.

WAR DIARY
or
~~INTELLIGENCE SUMMARY~~ of 121st Field Coy. R.E.
(Erase heading not required.)

Army Form C. 2118.

Vol 14

Place	Date	Hour	Summary of Events and Information	Remarks and references to Appendices
Aldershot Camp T19b6 3 sheet 28 SW	1.11.16		HQ + No 3 sections billeted here Work - Improvement of Camp viz making roads - laying a small water supply filtered to Ablution House. Drainage of Camp by means of shallow drains. Transport drawing R.E. stores from De Seule dump to SOUVENIR DUMP	
De Kennebak Cabt	"		Nos 1 2 + 4 sections billeted here No 4 section working on Concrete shelters in Front line - 107 Bde area No 1 + 2 sections T M positions near SPRING WALK and at N 36 c 6 4½ - Elephant shelters at MACBRIDES MANSIONS + FORBES TERRACE Dressing stations at ST QUENTIN Cabt + CANDAHAR FARM construction of Trench tramway + bridges from De Kennebak Cabt to SOUVENIR FARM one man admitted to Hospital	H.G.

70

Instructions regarding War Diaries and Intelligence Summaries are contained in F. S. Regs., Part II. and the Staff Manual respectively. Title pages will be prepared in manuscript.

Secret

WAR DIARY of 121st Field Coy R.E.
or
~~INTELLIGENCE SUMMARY.~~
(Erase heading not required.)

Army Form C. 2118.

Place	Date	Hour	Summary of Events and Information	Remarks and references to Appendices
Aldershot Camp	2/11/16		Work proceeds as on 1st inst one man discharged from Hospital	
De Kennebeck Cabt	3/11/16		work as on 1st inst one man admitted F.A do - one Reinforcement joined Coy. one man evacuated	
"	4/11/16		work as on 1st inst	
"	5/11/16		do	
"	6/11/16		do - one man evacuated	
"	7/11/16		do - very heavy rain during the day	
"	8/11/16		work as on 1st inst. - one man admitted Hosp - one man evacuated Drainage of Camp Completed Weather has been exceptionally bad for the past week	
"	9/11/16		work as on 8th inst.	JH.

T2134. Wt. W708—776. 500000. 4/15. Sir J. C. & S.

71

Secret

Instructions regarding War Diaries and Intelligence Summaries are contained in F. S. Regs., Part II. and the Staff Manual respectively. Title pages will be prepared in manuscript.

WAR DIARY or ~~INTELLIGENCE SUMMARY~~.

(*Erase heading not required.*)

121st Field Coy R.E.

Army Form C. 2118.

Place	Date	Hour	Summary of Events and Information	Remarks and references to Appendices
Aldershot camp	10/11/16		work proceeds as on 8th inst - but no Inf working parties	HH
	11/11/16		"	HH
Dr Kenneth Coll.	12/11/16		" - In Camp work Double rows of trench boards are being laid and parts of Camp not in use wired off.	HH
	13/11/16		work as on 12th inst.	HH
	14/11/16		do	HH
"	15/11/16		do - weather has been exceptionally cold.	HH
"	16/11/16		work proceeds as on 12th inst.	HH
"	17/11/16		do do	HH
"	18/11/16		work was considerably curtailed owing to wet weather.	HH
"	19/11/16		(Sunday) work as on 12th inst.	
			One man evacuated 13th inst.	HH
			" Transferred from 122nd Field Coy R.E. 17.11.16	
			" rejoined Coy from 36th Divl Res. Coy	HH

T2134. Wt. W708–776. 500000. 4/15. Sir J. C. & S.

Secret

72

Instructions regarding War Diaries and Intelligence Summaries are contained in F. S. Regs., Part II. and the Staff Manual respectively. Title pages will be prepared in manuscript.

WAR DIARY or ~~INTELLIGENCE~~ SUMMARY. of 121st Field Coy R.E.

(*Erase heading not required.*)

Army Form C. 2118.

Place	Date	Hour	Summary of Events and Information	Remarks and references to Appendices
Aldershot Camp	20/11/16		Work continues as on 12th inst. – weather has improved a little.	JHG
+ De Kennebak Camp	21/11/16		work proceeds as on 12th inst.	JHG
	22/11/16		" – no working parties owing to Relief. An oil engine partially damaged being taken down ready for removal from WULVERGHEM.	JHG
"	23/11/16		work as on 12th inst. but had to cease at 11 am. owing to prearranged bombardment of enemy Trenches. Parts of Engine referred to were brought by Lorry to Second Army workshops. HAZEBROOK	JHG
"	24/11/16		work proceeds as on 12th inst. – More parts of engine ~~were~~ brought to Second Army workshops. Trench stores were brought by Transport from DRANOUTRE to DE KENNEBAK – ready for transport to trenches by Trench tramway	JHG

T2134. Wt. W708–776. 500000. 4/15. Sir J. C. & S.

73

Secret

Instructions regarding War Diaries and Intelligence Summaries are contained in F. S. Regs., Part II. and the Staff Manual respectively. Title pages will be prepared in manuscript.

WAR DIARY or ~~INTELLIGENCE~~ SUMMARY. 121st Field Coy R.E.

(Erase heading not required.)

Army Form C. 2118.

Place	Date	Hour	Summary of Events and Information	Remarks and references to Appendices
Aldershot Camp & De Kennebak Cabt	25/11/16		Work continues as on 12th inst - weather moderate.	HL
	26/11/16		do	HL
	27/11/16		do	HL
	28/11/16		do - no working parties owing to relief	HL
	29/11/16		Monthly holiday	HL
	30/11/16		Work as on 12th inst. Working parties withdrawn at 1.30pm owing to prearranged bombardment. The weather has been moderate for the past week but cold. 64455 Sapper Crawford W.S. was wounded by bullet 22nd inst.	HL

HLunch Lieut R.E.

O.C. 121st Field Coy R.E.

T2134. Wt. W708—776. 500000. 4/15. Sir J. C. & S.

Vol 15

Confidential

War Diary

of

121st Field Company R.E.

December 1916.

74

Instructions regarding War Diaries and Intelligence Summaries are contained in F. S. Regs., Part II. and the Staff Manual respectively. Title pages will be prepared in manuscript.

WAR DIARY
or of 121st Field Coy. R.E.
~~INTELLIGENCE SUMMARY~~.
(*Erase heading not required.*)

Army Form C. 2118.

Place	Date	Hour	Summary of Events and Information	Remarks and references to Appendices
Aldershot Camp	1.12.16		H.Q + No 3 sections billetted here	
			Work Laying road in camp - constructing forage store	S.E.S.
			Transport drawing R.E. stores from De Seule for work in Trenches.	
De Kennebak Cabt			Nos 1, 2 + 4 billetted here	S.E.S.
			Trench work	
			Repairs to Agnes St. + Spring Walk.	
			Construction of elephants at KANDAHAR FARM dressing station	S.E.S.
			" ST QUENTIN CABT. Battn HQ.	
			" Dugouts (Concrete) in front line 107 Bde area	
			" H.T. M position N 36 C 6 4½	
			MTM " off SPRINGWALK.	
			" Tramway DEKENNEBK CABT to SOUVENIR FARM.	
	2.12.16		Work as on 1st inst.	
	3.12.16		HQ + No 3 sections preparing for move - remainder work as on 1st	S.E.S.
	4.12.16		HQ + No 3 sections moved to MONMOUTHSHIRE CAMP vacated by	S.E.S.
			150th Field Coy R.E. map Ref. M 35 b 4 4 sheet 28 S.W.	S.E.S.

T2134. Wt. W708–776. 500000. 4/15. Sir J. C. & S.

75

Instructions regarding War Diaries and Intelligence Summaries are contained in F. S. Regs., Part II. and the Staff Manual respectively. Title pages will be prepared in manuscript.

WAR DIARY or ~~INTELLIGENCE~~ SUMMARY.

of 121st Field Coy R.E.

(Erase heading not required.)

Army Form C. 2118.

Place	Date	Hour	Summary of Events and Information	Remarks and references to Appendices
			DRANOUTRE	
MONMOUTHSHIRE CAMP	5.12.16		Running of Div^l Baths taken over. Also running of engine for water supply at M 29 c 45	J.E.S.
DeKENNEBAK Cabt.			Transport drawing R.E. Stores from De Seule to Souvenir Dump.	J.E.S.
			Trench work as usual but no working parties owing to Relief	
"	6.12.16		Work at HQ Construction of Rifle Range (miniature at) M 29 c 41. Working parties supplied by German Prisoners.	J.E.S.
			Repair of water supply at M 29 c 45	
			Alterations to Divisional Baths DRANOUTRE. Transport as on 5th	
"			Trench Work	
			As on 5th inst.	
"	7.12.16		Work as on 6th inst. - one man evacuated to C.C.S.	J.E.S.
"	8.12.16		do - one man admitted Hosp.	J.E.S.
"	9.12.16		do	
"	10.12.16		do	
"	11.12.16		Holiday - Drill in forenoon	J.E.S.
"	12.12.16		Work as on 6th inst with addition of Repairs to Cinema Hall DRANOUTRE	J.E.S.
				J.E.S.

2353 Wt. W2544/1454 700,000 5/15 D. D. & L. A.D.S.S. Forms/C. 2118.

76

Instructions regarding War Diaries and Intelligence Summaries are contained in F. S. Regs., Part II. and the Staff Manual respectively. Title pages will be prepared in manuscript.

WAR DIARY or ~~INTELLIGENCE~~ SUMMARY.

121st Field Coy R.E.

(Erase heading not required.)

Army Form C. 2118.

Place	Date	Hour	Summary of Events and Information	Remarks and references to Appendices
MONMOUTH Camp + DEKENNEBAK Cabt	13.12.16		Work at MONMOUTH CAMP as on 12th inst.	J.E.S.
			Trench work as on 12th inst. One man evacuated 11th inst.	J.E.S.
	14.12.16		Work continues as on 13th inst.	
	15.12.16		do	J.E.S.
	16.12.16		Holiday for detachment at DEKENNEBAK (Drill in presence)	J.E.S.
			Work at H.Q. as on 13th inst. Three men admitted hospital	J.E.S.
	17.12.16		Work proceeds as on 13th inst. Additional work at H.Q. construction of Horsestandings – Ground for these being prepared by German prisoners	J.E.S.
	18.12.16		work as on 17th inst. One man evacuated 16.12.16 one man rejoined from Hospital. Parts of engine which had been salved near WULVERGHEM brought to HAZEBROUCK	J.E.S. J.E.S.
	19.12.16		work as on 17th inst. LIEUT. H. J. PALMER Seriously wounded by H.E. shell.	J.E.S.
	20.12.16		work as on 19th inst. The weather has been frosty + cold for the past few days.	J.E.S.

2353 Wt. W2544/1454 700,000 5/15 D. D. & L. A.D.S.S. Forms/C 2118.

77

Instructions regarding War Diaries and Intelligence Summaries are contained in F. S. Regs., Part II. and the Staff Manual respectively. Title pages will be prepared in manuscript.

Army Form C. 2118.

WAR DIARY
or
~~INTELLIGENCE~~ ~~SUMMARY.~~
(*Erase heading not required.*)

of 121st Field Coy R.E.

Place	Date	Hour	Summary of Events and Information	Remarks and references to Appendices
MONMOUTH CAMP. DE KENNEBAK	21.12.16		H.Q work - repairs to Divisional Baths DRANOUTRE Construction of Rifle Range at M 29 C 4) Preparation for construction of Horse standings at M 35 b 4 4 Trench work as on 12th inst.	JES
			Lieut H.J. PALMER died from wounds. 2 reinforcements joined Coy. one man admitted hosp.	JES
"	22.12.16		H.Q work as on 21st inst. No trench work owing to Relief.	JES
"	23.12.16		Work as on 21st inst. but no Infantry working parties 2 men discharged from hospital. one man evacuated. No 3 section relieved No 4 section from Trench work	JES
"	24.12.16		work as on 21st inst. One man discharged Hosp. one man admitted hospital.	JES
"	25.12.16		XMAS DAY. - no work. Coy had a very good supply of extras bought from Canteen funds & all enjoyed the day. One officer reinforcement joined Coy 2 Lt. Whyte	
"	26.12.16		H.Q work Repairs to Divisional Baths sawing timber erection of Nissen huts for Baths Trench work as on 21st inst.	JES

2353 Wt. W2544/1454 700,000 5/15 D. D. & L. A.D.S.S. Forms/C 2118.

Instructions regarding War Diaries and Intelligence Summaries are contained in F. S. Regs., Part II. and the Staff Manual respectively. Title pages will be prepared in manuscript.

WAR DIARY or ~~INTELLIGENCE SUMMARY~~. of 121st Field Coy R.E.

(Erase heading not required.)

Army Form C. 2118.

Place	Date	Hour	Summary of Events and Information	Remarks and references to Appendices
MONMOUTH CAMP +	27/12/16		work as on 26th inst. one man discharged hospital one man killed + one man wounded by T. M. (Killed 57734 Sapper McWilliams R wounded 64142 Sapper Taylor J.B.)	[illegible]
DEKENNEBAK	28/12/16		no trench work owing to Relief.	[illegible]
	29/12/16		Work as on 26th inst but no working parties one man discharged from hospital	[illegible]
	30/12/16		work as on 26th inst. one officer reinforcement joined Coy (Lieut C. P. Almond) 36th Divisional Order No. 1388 of 29th inst. states. "In future the NEUVE EGLISE road Baths and Laundry will be called the PALMER Baths to commemorate the work done by the late Lieutenant PALMER who was killed by a German shell at WULVERGHEM."	[illegible]
"	31/12/16		work as on 26th inst 131047 Sapper Kneeshaw R killed 64105 " Corpl Greer W. wounded by T. M today	[illegible]

[signature] Major, R.E.
O.C. 121st Field Coy., R.E.

2353 Wt. W2544/1454 700,000 5/15 D. D. & L. A.D.S.S. Forms/C. 2118.

original

Confidential Vol 16

WAR DIARY

of

O.C. 121st. Field Coy R.E.

From 1/1/17 to 31/1/17.

79

Instructions regarding War Diaries and Intelligence Summaries are contained in F. S. Regs., Part II. and the Staff Manual respectively. Title pages will be prepared in manuscript.

WAR DIARY or ~~INTELLIGENCE SUMMARY.~~

of 121st Field Coy R.E.

(Erase heading not required.)

Army Form C. 2118.

Place	Date	Hour	Summary of Events and Information	Remarks and references to Appendices
Monmouth Camp M35b 4 4 & De Kennebak T 3 central	1.1.17		Owing to withdrawal of 108 Inf Bde from line 107 Bde has extended its line to right taking over half of 108 Inf. Bde area. Work. Bde section (No 3 under 2 Lt J.S. Whyte R.E.) working on concrete dug outs in Front line. Nos. 1 & 2 sections - Repairs & improvements to communication & support trenches in area. Construction of 2 elephant dugouts at FORBES TERRACE. also 2 elephants at PETAWAWA FARM and at FISHER'S PLACE. HQ & No 4 sections billeted a MONMOUTH CAMP Work Construction of Horse standings at Camp Construction of stables for 8th 9th & 15th R I R at M30 C & d. " ration store harness room for 10th R I R Two men admitted hospital today	HL
"	2.1.17		Work as on 1st inst. - 64474 Sapper Francey J.A. proceeded to England to take up Commission (Temporary) in Infantry. 64019 Sapper Brown W. wounded by M.G. bullet.	HL

2353 Wt. W2544/1454 700,000 5/15 D. D. & L. A.D.S.S. Forms/C. 2118.

Instructions regarding War Diaries and Intelligence Summaries are contained in F. S. Regs., Part II. and the Staff Manual respectively. Title pages will be prepared in manuscript.

80

WAR DIARY or ~~INTELLIGENCE SUMMARY~~. 121st Field Coy. R.E.

(*Erase heading not required.*)

Army Form C. 2118.

Place	Date	Hour	Summary of Events and Information	Remarks and references to Appendices
MONMOUTH CAMP + DE KENNEBAK	3.1.17		Work as on 2nd inst. - one man evacuated to C.C.S.	HG
			New Years Honours	
			Captn. J.E. Stewart awarded Military Cross.	
			~~64238~~ Sergt. H McRoberts mentioned in despatches	
	4.1.17		work as on 3rd inst.	HG
			57675 Sapper McCaw. S. wounded by H.E.	
	5.1.17		work as on 4th inst. one admitted hospital	HG
	6.1.17		work as on 5th inst. - Lieut. C.T. Almond admitted hospl.	HG
	7.1.17		do 57103 CSM Warry proceeded to 36th Divisional School of Instruction as Instructor in Field Works	HG
	8.1.17		work as on 7th inst. - one man admitted hospital	HG
	9.1.17		Relief in 107 Bde area - no working parties supplied no front line work done by Coy. - one man admitted hospital	HG
	10.1.17		Work as on 8th inst. but no working parties supplied by Infantry. II Lieut J.S. Whyte buried by shell + admitted hospital suffering from shell shock. - 3 reinforcements joined Coy. Owing to very heavy shelling of forward area Nos 1 + 2 sections were withdrawn to Monmouth Camp from De Kennebak.	HG

T2134. Wt. W708—776. 500000. 4/15. Sir J. C. & S.

81/

Instructions regarding War Diaries and Intelligence Summaries are contained in F. S. Regs., Part II. and the Staff Manual respectively. Title pages will be prepared in manuscript.

WAR DIARY. or ~~INTELLIGENCE SUMMARY.~~ 121st Field Coy. R.E.

(*Erase heading not required.*)

Army Form C. 2118.

Place	Date	Hour	Summary of Events and Information	Remarks and references to Appendices
MONMOUTH CAMP. De Kennebak Cattle	11.1.17		Work as on 10th inst. one man discharged from hospital one man admitted hospital. Lieut A J Fawcett admitted hosp. 2 Lieut Deans 16th R.I.R. attached to Coy. for duty	Hy
"	12.1.17		work as on 11th inst. - one man admitted to hosp.	Hy
"	13.1.17		do do 57771 Corpl H.W. Anderson proceeded to England to take up Commission in Infantry	Hy
"	14.1.17		(Sunday) work as on 13th inst.	Hy
"	15.1.17		(Relief) No working parties + no R.E. work. one man admitted to Hospital. 2 Lieut J.T.V. Norman joined Coy. for duty.	Hy
"	16.1.17		work as on 14th inst. one man evacuated one man admitted Hospital. Two men discharged from Hospital	Hy
	17.1.17		work proceeds as on 16th inst. one man evacuated - 2 men discharged from hospital.	Hy
	18.1.17		Work as on 17th inst 3 reinforcements joined Coy	Hy

T2134. Wt. W708–776. 500000. 4/15. Sir J. C. & S.

82

Instructions regarding War Diaries and Intelligence Summaries are contained in F. S. Regs., Part II. and the Staff Manual respectively. Title pages will be prepared in manuscript.

WAR DIARY
of 121st Field Coy R.E.
~~INTELLIGENCE SUMMARY.~~
(*Erase heading not required.*)

Army Form C. 2118.

Place	Date	Hour	Summary of Events and Information	Remarks and references to Appendices
MONMOUTH Camp	19.1.17		Work as on 18th inst. 2 Lieut J. S. Whyte R.E. invalided to England	
			~~Work~~ as on 19th inst.	HL
(De Kennebak)	20.1.17		(Relief) - No working parties + no front line work.	HL
	21.1.17		Work as on 19th inst but no working parties	HL
	22.1.17		2 Lieut W.H. Blagden R.E. + 2 Lieut G.W.L. Day R.E. joined Coy. for duty work as on 20th inst	HL
	23.1.17		do. The weather for the past ten days has been very ~~cold~~, There has been snow + frost - Frost still Continues.	HL
"	24.1.17		Work continues as on 23rd inst.	HL
"	25.1.17		do	HL
"	26.1.17		Owing to 107 Bde withdrawing from the line this Coy moved into billets of 122nd Field Coy R.E. at PETIT PONT farm (T22b 22) - 122nd Field Coy R.E. took over the billets vacated by this Coy. - Our works were handed over to 122nd Field Coy R.E. The Coy is now in Divisional Reserve. The mounted portion moved to billets at ROMARIN (Sheet 36NW B4a93)	HL

T2134. Wt. W708—776. 500000. 4/15. Sir J. C. & S.

83

Instructions regarding War Diaries and Intelligence Summaries are contained in F. S. Regs., Part II. and the Staff Manual respectively. Title pages will be prepared in manuscript.

WAR DIARY of 121st Field Coy R.E.
or
~~INTELLIGENCE~~ SUMMARY.
(*Erase heading not required.*)

Army Form C. 2118.

Place	Date	Hour	Summary of Events and Information	Remarks and references to Appendices
PETIT PONT farm (T22 b 2.2)	27.1.17		Health & Kit Inspections – Checking stores in tool carts Hard frost continues. Lieut R.E. Walsh joined Coy on transfer from 1/2nd Pontoon Park	[initials]
	28.1.17		8 men detached for duty with 36 Div^l Hutting Coy. Work – Improvements to Horse Lines at ROMARIN Repair to Water supply at MONT NOIR. Wiring & improvement of Trenches at U 13 (28 S.W.) Construction of Gun positions at " " Bridges for Trench Tramway at T 17 + 23 (sheet 28 S.W.) to Gun positions	[initials]
	29.1.17		Work as on 28th. Lieut J.A. Wilson transferred to No 9 Pontoon Park R.E. Two reinforcements joined Coy.	[initials]
	30.1.17		Work as on 29th Captain R.A.H. Lewin transferred from 42nd AT Coy R.E. & assumed Command of this Coy.	[initials]
	31.1.17		Work as on 30th. Captn J.G. Stewart proceeded to Rouen to act as Instructor at R.E. Training Camp	[initials]

[signature] Capt. R.E.
O.C. 121st Field Coy, R.E.

T2134. Wt. W708—776. 500000. 4/15. Sir J. C. & S.

Confidential

Vol 17

WAR DIARY

of.

O.C. 121 Field Coy R.E.

February 1917.

Instructions regarding War Diaries and Intelligence Summaries are contained in F. S. Regs., Part II. and the Staff Manual respectively. Title pages will be prepared in manuscript.

WAR DIARY
or
~~INTELLIGENCE SUMMARY.~~
(Erase heading not required.)

Army Form C. 2118.

SECRET

Place	Date	Hour	Summary of Events and Information	Remarks and references to Appendices
PETIT PONT.	1/2/17		H.Q. Billet at PETIT PONT farm. Mounted Section at ROMARIN. Company employed on 4.5 How* concrete emplacements at U13d91 & 18 Pr concrete emplacements at T17d25. Wiring in front of Subsidiary Line T12. Repairing HEATH TRENCH T13b 2.6. Repairs to Church Army Hut RED LODGE. Hutting at ST MARIE CAPELLE, ALDERSHOT CAMP, WATERLOO ROAD CAMP. Wiring in front of HILL 63 Forts T18 a & b. Repairs to Water Supply MONT NOIR Officers Rest Station. Working of PALMER BATHS. Ground very hard through frost. No. Inf: One M.A.H.* One M.R.H (*)	MM
	2/2/17		Work as above. One M.A.H. No. Inf:	MM
	3/2/17		Work as above. No Inf.	MM
	4/2/17		~~Work as above.~~ One M.A.H. No work. Drill, inspection of gas helmets, box respirators etc. No Inf:	MM
	5/2/17		Work as usual. Heavy frost still continuing. No Inf.	MM
	6/2/17		Work as above. 57103 C.S.M. WARRY rejoined from Div^l School. No Inf.	MM
	7/2/17		Work as above. Emergency pumping arrangements started operating for PALMER BATHS. Dam at DRANOUTRE BATHS repaired. No Inf.	MM

* Man Admitted to Hospital. (*) Man Rejoined from Hospital.

T2134. Wt. W708—776. 500000. 4/15. Sir J. C. & S.

WAR DIARY
or
~~INTELLIGENCE SUMMARY.~~
(Erase heading not required.)

Army Form C. 2118.

Instructions regarding War Diaries and Intelligence Summaries are contained in F. S. Regs., Part II. and the Staff Manual respectively. Title pages will be prepared in manuscript.

Place	Date	Hour	Summary of Events and Information	Remarks and references to Appendices
	8/2/17		Work as above No 64222 Sgt McNeill proceeded to England to take up Temporary Commission. No Inf.	[illegible]
	9/2/17		Work as above. One M.A.H. No Inf.	[illegible]
	10/2/17		Work as above. Two M.R.H. No Inf.	[illegible]
	11/2/17		No work. Drill & inspections. No Inf.	[illegible]
	12/2/17		Work as usual. Ballasting & repairs to L'ALOUETTE Tramway started. No Inf.	[illegible]
	13/2/17		As above. No Inf.	[illegible]
	14/2/17		As above. No 4 Section proceeded to PONT DE ST QUENTIN dug outs T 5 d 9 4 for work on constructing dug Brigade H.Q. dugout at T 6 a 5 9. No Inf.	[illegible]
	15/2/17		Work as above. Bde H.Q. dug out started. Part of NEUVE EGLISE – WULVERGHEM road screened. 10 Inf.	[illegible]
	16/2/17		Work as above. Thaw set in, & thaw restrictions imposed for 6 days. 20. Inf.	[illegible]
	17/2/17		As above. 45 Inf.	[illegible]
	18/2/17		No work except for one small party wiring. Drills, inspections etc. 25 Inf.	[illegible]
	19/2/17		Work as usual. 95 Inf.	[illegible]
	20/2/17		As above 95. Inf.	[illegible]
	21/2/17		As above. 95 Inf. One man evacuated to C.C.S.	[illegible]
	22/2/17		As above. 70 Inf.	[illegible]

T2134. Wt. W708–776. 500000. 4/15. Sir J. C. & S.

Army Form C. 2118.

WAR DIARY
or
~~INTELLIGENCE SUMMARY.~~
(Erase heading not required.)

Instructions regarding War Diaries and Intelligence Summaries are contained in F. S. Regs., Part II. and the Staff Manual respectively. Title pages will be prepared in manuscript.

Place	Date	Hour	Summary of Events and Information	Remarks and references to Appendices
	23/2/17		Work as usual. 40 2/. Orders received to exchange work with 150 Coy RE on occasion of Brigade Relief.	AMR
	24/2/17		Last day of work on existing work. Officers, N.C.O's & men from both Coys interchanged in the handing over of work 40 2/	AMR
	25/2/17		No work. Drills, inspection etc. No 4 section rejoined Hdqrs. Relief ~~[illegible]~~ completed No 2/	AMR
	26/2/17		Coy work as follows. 12 Strong Points in front line over Brigade front. Draining & deep dugouts at ~~[illegible]~~ ~~[illegible]~~ ADVANCED ESTAMINET. Repairing CURRIE AV: & WINNIPEG AV:. Completing LOCALITY 3. Reclaiming WINNIPEG AV: ~~[illegible]~~ between WINTER TRENCH & REGINA CUT OFF. Reclaiming HAMBURY SUPPORT SOUTH. Continuing M.T.M. Emplacement in left sub sector front line, R.A.P at T7 b 5 6, & R.A.P at T14 c 8 5.	
			Work continued ~~[illegible]~~ at HEATH TRENCH, & wiring HILL 63 posts. 70 2/	AMR
	27/2/17		Work as above. 460 2/ Two M.A.H.	AMR
	28/2/17		Work as above. 360. 2/ Two M.A.H. One man evacuated.	AMR

[signature] Maj. RE.
O.C. 121st Field Coy RE

T2134. Wt. W708—776. 500000. 4/15. Sir J. C. & S.

Confidential

Vol 18

War Diary

of.

O.C. 121 Field Coy R.E.

for month of March 1917.

SECRET

Army Form C. 2118

Instructions regarding War Diaries and Intelligence Summaries are contained in F. S. Regs., Part II. and the Staff Manual respectively. Title Pages will be prepared in manuscript.

WAR DIARY of 121st Field Coy RE

(Erase heading not required.)

Place	Date	Hour	Summary of Events and Information	Remarks and references to Appendices
PETIT PONT	1/3/17		Hdqrs + 4 Sections. Mounted Section at ROMARIN Coy employed at construction of Strong Points in the front line; repairs to all CT's + their maintenance in the Brigade area; revetting HEATH TRENCH - N. end; joining WINNIPEG AV: to WINTER TRENCH; completing concrete M.G.E in Subs: Line; draining 4 concrete dug-outs ADVi ESTAMINET; completing 1st Aid Post HALFWAY HOUSE; and at WELL LANE; reclaiming HAMBURY SUPPORT SOUTH; constructing 3 dug-outs in the Front Line. 350 Inf: One M.A.H. One M.E.	
	2/3/17		Rest day for ½ Coy. Work as above. 360 Inf:	
	3/3/17		Work as above. 360 Inf:	
	4/3/17		Work as above. 1 Section rest day. 200 Inf: One M.A.H	
	5/3/17		Work as above. 260 Inf One M.A.H.	
	6/3/17		Work as above 260 Inf:	121st COY. ROYAL ENGINEERS No. 5218 Date 2/4/17 ULSTER DIVISION
	7/3/17		As above. 260 Inf: Lieut. W.H. BLAGDEN R.E attached to 150 Coy: RE.	
	8/3/17		As above. 1 Section rest day. 260 Inf:	

1875 Wt. W593/826 1,000,000 4/15 J.B.C. & A. A.D.S.S./Forms/C. 2118.

SECRET

Army Form C. 2118.

Instructions regarding War Diaries and Intelligence Summaries are contained in F. S. Regs., Part II. and the Staff Manual respectively. Title pages will be prepared in manuscript.

WAR DIARY or ~~INTELLIGENCE SUMMARY~~ of 121st Field Coy RE

(Erase heading not required.)

Place	Date	Hour	Summary of Events and Information	Remarks and references to Appendices
PETIT PONT	9/3/17		Work as above. 1 section rest day. Instructions received to show 1st Field Coy N.Z.E all work, preparatory to handing over. 260 Inf:	
	10/3/17		Work as above. 1 section rest day. 260 Inf:	
	11/3/17		Work as above. 200 Inf: No 64616 Spr Burnell wounded, & remains at duty.	
	12/3/17		N.Z.E officially take over all work. 4 section sergeants go round new (16th Div.) sector. One M.R.H. No Inf: Lieut R.E. WALSH R.E. admitted to hospital.	
	13/3/17		Nos 1 & 4 sections moved to BUS FARM and Nos 2 & 3 with Hdqrs to LURGAN CAMP.	
LURGAN CAMP	14/3/17		Work on billets. No Inf: One reinforcement joined. One M.R.H.	
	15/3/17		Carpenters of 2 & 3 sections moved to BUS FARM for work. Expansion of BUS FARM billet to ~~[illegible]~~ accomodate 4 sections. Two M.E. No Inf:	
	16/3/17		Started work on erecting Baby Elephant shelters in Front Line; revetting LONG LANE & building up parapet; draining ULSTER ROAD; new Coy H.Q. - 5.9 concrete dug out ~~at~~ PICCADILLY N25 d 35.40; converting elephants of R.A.P. BUS FARM. Billet improvements & expansion of BUS FARM. 20 Inf: One M.R.H	
	17/3/17		Work as above. Remainder of Nos 2 & 3 sections moved to BUS FARM. 140 Inf: Fixing bunks etc in S.P.6	
	18/3/17		Work as above. Mounted men moved from ROMARIN to LURGAN CAMP, with all transport etc. 140 Inf: Started wiring S.P.6 & 7; ballasting Trench Tramway from R.E. FARM & PICCADILLY LOOP:	

2353 Wt. W2544/1454 700,000 5/15 D. D. & L. A.D.S.S./Forms/C. 2118.

SECRET

Army Form C. 2118.

Instructions regarding War Diaries and Intelligence Summaries are contained in F. S. Regs., Part II. and the Staff Manual respectively. Title pages will be prepared in manuscript.

WAR DIARY or ~~INTELLIGENCE~~ SUMMARY. of 121st Field Coy R.E.

(Erase heading not required.)

Place	Date	Hour	Summary of Events and Information	Remarks and references to Appendices
ORGAN CAMP	19/3/17		Work as above. New M.G.E called CROWN POST started, N28C83; fitting in of 4 shelters in S.P.8 started; 80 Inf:	
	20/3/17		Work as above. 410 Inf.	
	21/3/17		Work as above. New M.G.E at POND FARM. N34d59 started. 480 Inf. Sergt SYKES quitted unit for England (commission)	
	22/3/17		Work as above. Wiring started between CROWN POST & BUS FARM. 480 Inf. Bn M.R.H.	
	23/3/17		As above. M.G.E CROWN POST transferred to 150 Coy RE. 480 Inf:	
	24/3/17		As above. 480 Inf: II Lieut W.H. BLAGDEN R.E rejoined from 150 Coy RE.	
	25/3/17		No work. Coy rest day. No Inf:	
	26/3/17		Work as usual. M.G dugout at VINE CORNER N35a8.8 started. 340 Inf: Wiring started S of POND FARM	
	27/3/17		Work as above. 410 Inf:	
	28/3/17		Work as above. M.G dugout at KINGSWAY N.35b3.0 started. 410 Inf	
	29/3/17		Work as above 410 Inf	
	30/3/17		Work as above 410 Inf:	
	31/3/17		No work as above. Coy rest day, except ½ section. Wiring A line with 1 Coy 13 R.I.R. started. 120 Inf:	

[illegible] Major RE
O C 121st Field Coy RE

2/4/17

121st COY. ROYAL ENGINEERS No. S218 Date 2/4/17 ULSTER DIVISION

T2134. Wt. W708—776. 500000. 4/15. Sir J. C. & S.

Confidential.

Vol 19

War Diary

of

O.C. 121 Field Coy. R.E.

From 1st April 1917 to 30th April 1917

Instructions regarding War Diaries and Intelligence Summaries are contained in F. S. Regs., Part II. and the Staff Manual respectively. Title pages will be prepared in manuscript.

WAR DIARY or INTELLIGENCE SUMMARY.

of 121st Field Coy R.E.

(Erase heading not required.)

Army Form C. 2118.

Place	Date	Hour	Summary of Events and Information	Remarks and references to Appendices
Lurgan Camp	1 4/17		Mounted portion with 10 Sappers billeted at Lurgan Camp Map Refa M35 d. 7.9. Sheet 28 S.W.	
Bus Farm			Sections 1, 2, 3, 4 billeted at Bus Farm N 33 d 4.1.	
			Work in line consisted of Construction of Concrete M.G.E & Dug-out at Pond Farm and concreted (Baby Elephants) dug-outs in Kingsway, Vine Corner and S.P.8. Wiring A & B lines, reclaiming of A line near SP8, digging and revetting trench to REDAN. AV and LONG. C.T. Construction of Concreted Coy H.Q. near support line.	
			Working Party of 13 Platoons. one M.D.H.	
	2 4/17		Work in line as above. Improvements to Lurgan Camp put in hand. Repairs to pipe line to ablution shed, concreting floors of latrines. Working party 13 Platoons	
	3 4/17		Work in line & in Camp as above. Working party 13 Platoons. Sgt Fowlie Transferred to Rly Transport depot	
	4 4/17		" " " " " L/Cpl Easton " " "	
	5 4/17		" " " " " 7 " 1 M.A.H. 3 Sapper reinforcements joined Coy	
	6 4/17		" " " " " 3 " Coy HQ completed. 1 Pioneer Coy took over some trench work	
	7 4/17		" " " " " 4 " 1 & 4 Sections had a day off. 1 M.D.H.	
	8 4/17		" " " no working party. 1 MDH. 2 + 3 Sections had a day off	
	9 4/17		" " " working party 3 Platoons 2 MAH. 1 MDH. 1 Reinforcement NCO joined	
	10 4/17		" " " Reclaiming old trench Cos part of GEORGE St Commenced. Working party 13 platoons of 8th R.I.R. 1 MAH.	

Army Form C. 2118.

Instructions regarding War Diaries and Intelligence Summaries are contained in F. S. Regs., Part II. and the Staff Manual respectively. Title pages will be prepared in manuscript.

WAR DIARY of INTELLIGENCE SUMMARY.

121st Field Coy R.E.

(Erase heading not required.)

Place	Date	Hour	Summary of Events and Information	Remarks and references to Appendices
	11/4/17		Work as above except that wiring of A line discontinued. Mtd Sgt Preston transferred from 2nd Pontoon Park. Working party 13 platoons	
	12/4/17		Work as above. Cpl White V.S. joined depot of F.S. Coys G.H.Q. 6 Reinforcements arrived. Working party 13 platoons	
	13/4/17		" " " " " 2 M.D.H. 1 Man wounded	
	14/4/17		" " " " " 1 M.A.H. 1 Reinforcement joined Coy	
	15/4/17		All sections had a days rest. 1 M.A.H. No working parties.	
	16/4/17		Work in line consisted of finishing off Pond Farm M.G.E., laying + screening of new KINGSWAY LINE (Trench Tramway) digging + revetting the following C.Ts REDAN. AV. GEORGE ST. VIGO ST. DUG-OUTS mention above were completed. Working Party 1 Platoon from 9th R. Innis Fus. 1 M.A.H.	
	17/4/17		Work as above. Working party 1 platoon. 1 M.D.H. 10 men awarded 1st G.C. badge.	
	18/4/17		" " " " " "	
	19/4/17		" " " " " "	
	20/4/17		" " " " " " 1 M.D.H.	
	21/4/17		" " " " " 9 platoons	
	22/4/17		" " " " " 9 "	

Instructions regarding War Diaries and Intelligence Summaries are contained in F. S. Regs., Part II. and the Staff Manual respectively. Title pages will be prepared in manuscript.

WAR DIARY
or
INTELLIGENCE SUMMARY.
(Erase heading not required.)

121st Field Coy R.E.

Army Form C. 2118.

Place	Date	Hour	Summary of Events and Information	Remarks and references to Appendices
"	23 4/17		Work as above. W.P. of 9 platoons. 1.M.A.H. Cpl McPhail transferred as Sergeant to No 8 Tramway Coy RE.	
	24 4/17		Work as on 23rd. Larger proportion of men put on night work owing to hostile sniping. 2 men wounded by HE. 1 L.D. horse destroyed debility.	
	25 4/17		Rest day for sappers. No W.P's. 1 MAH. Wagons being re painted. Quantity of trench name plates for 'Hunland' prepared.	
	26 4/17		Work as on 24th. 2 MAH. 1 MDH.	
	27 4/17		— " — 3 Reinforcements joined.	
	28 4/17		— " — W.P's reduced by 20 men. 1 MDH.	
	29 4/17		(Sunday) usual afternoon holiday for drivers. Work in line as on 28th.	1. M.A.H.
	30 4/17		Work as yesterday for sappers. Hostile shelling considerably interfered with work. Preparations in progress for Divl Horse Show.	

2/5/17

H. Crock[?] Capt RE
OC. 121st (Field) Coy. RE

2353 Wt. W2544/1454 700,000 5/15 D. D. & L. A.D.S.S. Forms/C 2118.

Confidential

Vol 20

WAR DIARY

of

O.C. 121 Field Coy R.E.

for month of MAY 1917.

Instructions regarding War Diaries and Intelligence Summaries are contained in F. S. Regs., Part II. and the Staff Manual respectively. Title Pages will be prepared in manuscript.

WAR DIARY
or
~~INTELLIGENCE SUMMARY~~
(Erase heading not required.)

Army Form C. 2118

Place	Date	Hour	Summary of Events and Information	Remarks and references to Appendices
LURGAN CAMP	1/5/17		Mounted section & 10 Sappers billetted at LURGAN CAMP. 4 Sections billetted at BUS FARM. Company was employed on ~~—~~ revetting REDAN AV: between S.P 7 & DEADMANS FARM; reclaiming & trench boarding GEORGE ST from BEEHIVE DUGOUTS to VINE CORNER; reclaiming new VIGO ST from PICCADILLY to Front Line. 9 platoons Inf: (13th R.I.R.) Exceptionally fine weather. No 3 Section screening & making formation for new Trench Tramway (KINGSWAY Line)	AMM
	2/5/17		Work as above. Same as above. 3 M.A.H.	AMM
	3/5/17		Rest day. Company attended Gas School demonstration. One M.R.H.	AMM
	4/5/17		Work as usual. Excavation started of THE STRAND. Same Inf: Two reinforcements	AMM
	5/5/17		As above. Same Inf: One M.R.H. All Coy: horses clipped.	AMM
	6/5/17		As above. Lieut WALSH took over No 3 Section. Same Inf: Alterations to POND FARM M.G.E started.	AMM
	7/5/17		As above. Same Inf: Divl Horse Show.	AMM
	8/5/17		As above. Same Inf: Two reinforcements. Two M.A.H.	AMM
	9/5/17		As above. Same Inf: Two M.A.H	AMM

1875 Wt. W593/826 1,000,000 4/15 J.B.C. & A. A.D.S.S./Forms/C. 2118.

Instructions regarding War Diaries and Intelligence Summaries are contained in F. S. Regs., Part II. and the Staff Manual respectively. Title Pages will be prepared in manuscript.

WAR DIARY
or
~~INTELLIGENCE SUMMARY~~
(Erase heading not required.)

Army Form C. 2118

Place	Date	Hour	Summary of Events and Information	Remarks and references to Appendices
	10/5/17		As above. POND FARM M.G.E. completed. Same Inf: Four M.A.H.	AM
	11/5/17		As above. Same Inf. Two M.R.H. One man evacuated.	AM
	12/5/17		As above. 13th R.I.R. ceased work. Two M.R.H. One M.A.H	AM
	13/5/17		As above. No Inf: Two M.R.H.	AM
	14/5/17		As above, 10. Platoons 9th Inn: Fus. One man evacuated. Three reinforcements.	AM
	15/5/17		As above. 2 New Battn H.Q dugouts (concrete) started near BEEHIVE Dugouts; small concrete Elephant	
	~~15/5/17~~		dugout started for wireman at VINE CORNER. Same Inf. One M.R.H. One M.A.H.	AM
	16/5/17		As above. Same Inf: Two M.A.H. Two M.R.H. One man evacuated.	AM
	17/5/17		As above. Same Inf: One M.R.H.	AM
	18/5/17		As above. Same Inf.	AM
	19/5/17		As above. Same Inf: Permanent Inf: party of 1 officer + 100 men from 107 Inf: Bde attached — bivouaced ~~of~~ on KEMMEL HILL.	AM
	20/5/17		As above. Same Inf: One M.R.H. Started flooring of In + Out boards of trenches.	AM

Instructions regarding War Diaries and Intelligence Summaries are contained in F. S. Regs., Part II. and the Staff Manual respectively. Title Pages will be prepared in manuscript.

WAR DIARY
or
~~INTELLIGENCE SUMMARY~~
(Erase heading not required.)

Army Form C. 2118

M. A. H — Man Admitted Hospital
M. R. H. — Man Rejoined from Hospital

Place	Date	Hour	Summary of Events and Information	Remarks and references to Appendices
	21/5/17		As above. Same Inf: Stocking the intermediate dump commenced. One M.R.H. Seven reinforcements.	RM
	22/5/17		As above. Same Inf: Work on Reserve Water Supply started.	RM
	23/5/17		As above. Same Inf: Name boards to complete all trenches, erected. Overland routes sited. Two M.R.H.	RM
	24/5/17		As above. Same Inf: BOW STR, STRAND & REDAN AV: completed. Work started on overland routes. One man evacuated.	RM
	25/5/17		As above. Same Inf: GEORGE ST completed. Two M.A.H.	RM
	26/5/17		As above. VIGO ST completed. Stormans dug-out at VINE CORNER completed. Same Inf: Two M.A.H.	RM
	27/5/17		As above. Same Inf: Strengthening BUS FARM billets. Two M.A.H. One M.R.H Horselines & billets at LURGAN CAMP shelled by night. Lieut A.J. FAWCETT R.E joined unit.	RM
	28/5/17		As above. Same Inf: Lieut G.W.L. DAY attached to 150 Coy RE.	RM
	29/5/17		As above. Same Inf: Night shelling in vicinity. One M.A.H. Two men evacuated.	RM
	30/5/17		As above. Same Inf: Night shelling of ~~vicinity~~ billet. 2 horses killed, 3 wounded. One M.R.H. One M.A.H.	RM
	31/5/17		As above. Same Inf: Night shelling of ~~billet~~ vicinity. ~~[illegible]~~. Sapper Jones. Drs Burnside & Gibson wounded by shrapnel in forward area. One M.R.H.	RM

RM Lewin Maj RE
O.C. 121st Field Coy RE.
1/6/17

121st COY. ROYAL ENGINEERS No. 5436 Date 1/6/17 ULSTER DIVISION

1875 Wt. W593/826 1,000,000 4/15 J.B.C. & A. A.D.S.S./Forms/C. 2118.

Vol 21

Confidential

War Diary

– of –

121st Field Coy R.E.

June, 1917.

Instructions regarding War Diaries and Intelligence Summaries are contained in F. S. Regs., Part II. and the Staff Manual respectively. Title Pages will be prepared in manuscript.

WAR DIARY

121st Field Company

~~INTELLIGENCE SUMMARY~~

(Erase heading not required.)

Army Form C. 2118

Place	Date	Hour	Summary of Events and Information	Remarks and references to Appendices
In the field Kurgan Camp. Dranoutre.	1/6/17		Work consisted of clearing cross country tracks to the assembly trenches, construction of Reserve Batt^n H.Q. at BEEHIVE DUG-OUTS, laying of KINGSWAY Tram-line, concrete O.P. in S.P.8, tarpaulin reservoir near DAYLIGHT CORNER, internal fittings of Bde and Batt^n battle H.Q. at SP6, SP7 and REGENT DUGOUTS, stocking of forward dumps. Working parties 13 Platoons. H.Q. Camp shelled at night. 4 Section of sappers on attachment at BUS FARM.	AMM
	2/6/17		Work as above. Painting of the pontoon wagons commenced. Iron frames, to carry barbed wire on pack animals, made. Direction boards for forward area painted. 2 men wounded and 1 man sent to hospital. Working party 4 platoons of attached Infantry. Tank for reserve supply of water erected at Bde H.Q. Half barrels for water erected on Kingsway Trench.	AMM
	3/6/17		Work as on 1/6/17. Tramline, OP and reservoir completed. 3 men wounded.	AMM
	4/6/17		4 Stretcher men (1 per section) Stocking of forward dumps and clearing cross country tracks continued. Forward billets (BUS FARM) improved & strengthened.	AMM
	5/6/17		Stocking of forward dumps completed. Cross Country tracks finished. One man accidently wounded by rifle grenade.	AMM
	6/6/17		12 mules with packsaddles sent forward to BUS FARM.	AMM
BUS FARM	7/6/17		Previous instructions had been received that each section would have to consolidate a strong point on the day of assault of WYTSCHAETE – MESSINES ridge. Orders were received at 8.30 am to proceed to consolidate S.P.6 (O25d 90.83), & at 9.0am to consolidate S.P.10 (O26d 25.80), S.P.11 (O26b 05.50) and S.P.12 (O26a 40.50)	

1875 Wt. W593/826 1,000,000 4/15 J.B.C. & A. A.D.S.S./Forms/C. 2118.

Instructions regarding War Diaries and Intelligence Summaries are contained in F. S. Regs., Part II. and the Staff Manual respectively. Title Pages will be prepared in manuscript.

WAR DIARY

121st Field ~~or~~ Company.

~~INTELLIGENCE SUMMARY~~

(Erase heading not required.)

Army Form C. 2118

Place	Date	Hour	Summary of Events and Information	Remarks and references to Appendices
BUS FARM	7/6/17		All sections moved off independently to the Intermediate dump VINE CORNER, the section having attached 22 Inf: and 3 pack mules. Every sapper, infantry man & mule loaded up stores here. All sections moved forward across country to their objectives. S.P's 6 & 12 were started at 11.45 am; & S.P's 10 & 11 at 12.15 pm. Each S.P was finished to the following scale. Frontal & flank fire trench (traversed) for one platoon, 2 flanking M.G.E at either flank, slit trenches for M.G crews & Infantry garrison, wired all round with a double top wire, strengthened by 60 yds French & barbed wire on each flank. Sections on completion of work they were capable of doing, returned to BUS FARM. Enemy interference on march up & back was negligible. Unaimed shell fire interfered slightly with S.P's 6, 10, 12. The heaviness of the load, & the heat of the day, very considerably lessened powers of working. 2nd Cpl Busby was killed at S.P 10; two sappers wounded.	NM
	8/6/17		Sections moved independently to the BLUE LINE taking wiring stores with attached Infantry, & 16 mules, & erected continuous belt of wire from O 25 b 8.4 to O 26 c 3.4, leaving BUS FARM at 2.0 pm, & returning 10.0 pm. No enemy interference.	NM

1875 Wt. W593/826 1,000,000 4/15 J.B.C. & A. A.D.S.S./Forms/C. 2118.

Instructions regarding War Diaries and Intelligence Summaries are contained in F. S. Regs., Part II. and the Staff Manual respectively. Title pages will be prepared in manuscript.

WAR DIARY
or
~~INTELLIGENCE SUMMARY.~~
(Erase heading not required.)

Army Form C. 2118.

Place	Date	Hour	Summary of Events and Information	Remarks and references to Appendices
LURGAN CAMP.	9/6/17		Whole Det^t at BUS FARM rejoined remainder of Coy at LURGAN CAMP. Billets at BUS FARM handed over to 67 Field Coy RE. Attached Inf: rejoined their Battalions.	AMR
	10/6/17		Coy drill, & inspections. One M.R.H.	AMR
	11/6/17		Coy drill & inspections. One M.A.H.	AMR
	12/6/17		Coy drill & inspections.	AMR
	13/6/17		1 Off: + 112 Inf: joined for attachment for proposed work on BLACK LINE. All sections moved to tents & bivouacs on KEMMEL HILL. One M.A.H.	AMR
	14/6/17		All sections and attached Inf: started wiring the BLACK LINE from LUMM POINT (O26d38) to O32d97 & improving existing trenches, draining etc. Working from 5.0 am to 10.0 am, weather hazy. Two M.A.H.	AMR
N35 a48	15/6/17		As above. Billets moved from KEMMEL HILL to N 35 a 4.8 taking tents & bivouacs. Three M.A.H.	AMR
	16/6/17		Work as above.	AMR
N34 b 2.6	17/6/17		Work as above. Camp moved back to 34 b 2.6 owing to enemy night shelling of bivouacs 2 nights in vicinity.	AMR
	18/6/17		Work as above. Last day of work on BLACK LINE. Orders received to move to R.E. FARM 35 d 5.6.	AMR
SHAMUS DUGOUTS	19/6/17		4 sections moved to R.E. FARM & SHAMUS DUGOUTS (35d 8.4); horse lines to BUS FARM. Both billets taken over from 67th Field Coy RE. Two M.A.H. One wounded.	AMR

2353 Wt. W2544/1454 700,000 5/15 D. D. & L. A.D.S.S./Forms/C. 2118.

Instructions regarding War Diaries and Intelligence Summaries are contained in F. S. Regs., Part II. and the Staff Manual respectively. Title Pages will be prepared in manuscript.

WAR DIARY

121st Field Company.

~~INTELLIGENCE SUMMARY~~

(Erase heading not required.)

Army Form C. 2118

Place	Date	Hour	Summary of Events and Information	Remarks and references to Appendices
SHAMUS DUGOUTS	20/6/17		By instructions received, two sections + half attached Inf. only to work daily. Work started by night, on wiring the ~~[illegible]~~ MAUVE LINE from O 27 b 07 to O 33 b 28, + improving roads between WYTSCHAETE – MESSINES road and MAUVE LINE, and making cross country tracks for wheeled transport.	AMM
	21/6/17		Work as above. 5 M.R.H.	AMM
	22/6/17		As above	AMM
	23/6/17		As above. 40775 Sgt. DYKE joined from the Base. One M.R.H.	AMM
	24/6/17		As above. L/Cpl WRIGHT wounded.	AMM
	25/6/17		As above. Two men evacuated.	AMM
	26/6/17		As above. One M.R.H. Three reinforcements	AMM
	27/6/17		As above. Last night of work, preparatory to move.	AMM
	28/6/17		No work. Cleaning up etc of camp, wagons etc. One M.R.H. One evacuated.	AMM
	29/6/17		As above. Orders received to march to WATOU next day.	AMM
WATOU.	30/6/17		Coy quitted billets at 3.40 am, delayed by shelling at LINDENHOEK; marched via KEMMEL + POPERINGHE to billets at WATOU arriving 9.30 am. Tents arrived 12.30 pm. Camp – H.Q + 4 Sections ~~at~~ 300 yds E of WATOU Church, + horse lines 600 yards S.W of WATOU church.	AMM

A M Mervin Maj RE
O.C 121st Field Coy RE.

1/7/17

121st COY. ROYAL ENGINEERS No. S 510 Date 1/7/17 ULSTER DIVISION

1875 Wt. W593/826 1,000,000 4/15 J.B.C. & A. A.D.S.S./Forms/C. 2118.

Vol 22

Confidential

WAR DIARY

of

OC. 121st. Field Coy. R.E.

For month of JULY 1917.

Army Form C. 2118.

Instructions regarding War Diaries and Intelligence Summaries are contained in F. S. Regs., Part II. and the Staff Manual respectively. Title pages will be prepared in manuscript.

WAR DIARY of 171st Field Coy R.E.
~~INTELLIGENCE~~ SUMMARY.

(Erase heading not required.)

Place	Date	Hour	Summary of Events and Information	Remarks and references to Appendices
WATOU	1/7/17		Dismounted men billeted at 27 E 28 d 6.0, horse lines at 27 L 5 a 4.4. Company employed on camp fatigues.	AM
	2/7/17		3 Sections employed on making frames & sets for wells. 1 Section started well at K 4 A 8.6. Gnr M.R.H.	AM
	3/7/17		Section carpenters on frames & sets. No 1 Section on well. Remainder drill. Gnr M.A.H.	AM
	4/7/17		As above. 2nd Section (2) started well at K 11 a 7.3. Gnr M.A.H.	AM
	5/7/17		As above. All men now required for well-work. – drill stopped.	AM
	6/7/17		As above. Well at K 4 a 8.6 completed. – 18' 6" deep.	AM
	7/7/17		As above. No 1 Section started well at K 6 b 7.2. Well at K 11 a 7.3 completed – 15' deep.	AM
	8/7/17		As above. No 2 Section started well at L 1 c 6.3.	AM
	9/7/17		As above. Barbed wire enclosure for Chinese compounds at L 8 b 9.5 & L 9 c 2.5 started.	AM
	10/7/17		As above. No 2 Section & 4 Section proceed to L 16 a 2.6 on detachment.	AM
	11/7/17		As above. Well at K 6 b 7.2 at 25', and L 1 c 6.3 at 20' both abandoned. Gnr M.A.H.	AM
	12/7/17		As above. No 3 Section started well at L 11 b 1.8, No 4 at L 16 a 0.6. No 3 Section proceed to Detmt ~~[illegible]~~. Enclosures at L 8 b 9.5 and L 9 c 2.5 completed. Gnr M.A.H.	AM

2353 Wt. W2544/1454 700,000 5/15 D. D. & L. A.D.S.S./Forms/C. 2118.

Army Form C. 2118.

Instructions regarding War Diaries and Intelligence Summaries are contained in F. S. Regs., Part II. and the Staff Manual respectively. Title pages will be prepared in manuscript.

WAR DIARY of 131st Field Coy RE. INTELLIGENCE SUMMARY.

(Erase heading not required.)

Place	Date	Hour	Summary of Events and Information	Remarks and references to Appendices
	13/7/17		As above. 3 reinforcements. Bottom & top fitted to wells at K4a 8.6, K11a 7 3, K5d 3.2 (Pioneers). L16a 0.6 Abandoned at 10'.	RMM
	14/7/17		As above. Well at L11b 1.8 completed – 11' 6" deep. Bottom & top to Pioneer wells at K12a 2.1, K5d 5.2, K13b 0.4. Bath house at E27 d 9.2 started.	
	~~14/7/17~~		~~As above~~ Abandoned wells at K6b 7.2, L1c 6.3, L16a 0.6 filled in. L11b 1.8 completed at 9' 6".	RMM
	15/7/17		As above. No 4 section started well at L15 d 9.1. Bottom & top fitted to Pioneer wells at K17b 2.1, L7d 2.3, L14c 5.2, No 3 section started well at L11a 7.6	RMM
	16/7/17		As above Bottom & top fitted to well at L11b 1.8. Started 30' x 30' canvas reservoir at L7d 6.2	RMM
	17/7/17		As above. Well at L11a 7.6 completed with bottom & top at 12' deep. One man evacuated. Sgt McRoberts awarded Croix de guerre.	RMM
	18/7/17		As above. One M.R.H. One evacuated. Three reinforcements. No 3 Section started 8' diam corrugated iron drum well at L14c 4.2. Started 11'x11' canvas reservoir at K3c 1.1. (P) Well at L9b 9.3 completed with bottom & top.	RMM
	19/7/17		As above. Well at L15d 9.1 completed. Bottom & top fitted to Pioneer wells at L9b 2.5, L14c 3.1. Reservoirs at L7d 6.2 & K3c 1.1 completed. Well at L16a 3.5 started (No 4 Section)	RMM
	20/7/17		As above. Well at L14c 4.2 completed with top & bottom. Bottom & top fitted to L15d 9.1. Well at L16a 3.5 completed with top & bottom	RMM
	21/7/17		As above. Started cook house & ablution shed for Chinese compound at L8b 9.5. Started erection of 48 horse troughs throughout the WATOU Area. Bath house at E27d 9.2 completed. One M.A.H.	RMM

2353 Wt. W2544/1454 700,000 5/15 D. D. & L. A.D.S.S./Forms/C. 2118.

Instructions regarding War Diaries and Intelligence Summaries are contained in F. S. Regs., Part II. and the Staff Manual respectively. Title pages will be prepared in manuscript.

WAR DIARY of 121st Field Coy RE ~~INTELLIGENCE SUMMARY.~~

(Erase heading not required.)

Army Form C. 2118.

Place	Date	Hour	Summary of Events and Information	Remarks and references to Appendices
"	22/7/17		As above. All carpentering work for wells finished. Bath house started at L14c 4.2 (No 3). One man evacuated.	RMM
	23/7/17		As above. No 1 Section started erection of 3 Nissen huts at K4d 2.2. Erection of Horse troughs finished. 2 reinforcements	RMM
	24/7/17		Ablution and cook house at L8b 95 finished. Work as above.	RMM
	25/7/17		Work as above. All sections on Det[nt] rejoined HQ at WATOU.	RMM
	26/7/17		As above. Nissen huts at K4d 2.2 completed.	RMM
	27/7/17		~~[illegible]~~ Bath house at L14c 42 finished. Sections squad & rifle drill. Practice in erection of trestle.	RMM
	28/7/17		Drill and practice in pontoon~~ing~~ bridging.	RMM
	29/7/17		Drill and practice in pontoon & trestle bridging.	RMM
	30/7/17		Striking camp & general fatigues. Coy marched at 10 pm for new camp at L16a 2.6	RMM
L16a 2.6	31/7/17		Coy arrived at 12.30 am. General fatigues, drill & inspection.	RMM

1/8/17.

R M Mewin Maj RE
O C 121st Field Coy RE

2353 Wt. W2544/1454 700,000 5/15 D. D. & L. A.D.S.S./Forms/C. 2118.

Confidential.

Vol 23

War Diary

of

121st Field Company R.E.

for month of August. 1917.

121st
FIELD COMPANY,
R.E.
No. S 615
Date 2/9/17

Instructions regarding War Diaries and Intelligence Summaries are contained in F. S. Regs., Part II. and the Staff Manual respectively. Title pages will be prepared in manuscript.

WAR DIARY

~~121st Field~~ ~~or Company~~. 121st Field Company

~~INTELLIGENCE SUMMARY.~~

(Erase heading not required.)

Army Form C. 2118.

SECRET

Place	Date	Hour	Summary of Events and Information	Remarks and references to Appendices
27 L 16 a 2.6	1/8/17		The whole unit together under canvas. No R.E. work being done. In readiness to move at 2 hours notice. 1 Officer + 100 O.R. Infantry joined for attachment	RM
	2/8/17		Instruction + drill.	RM
	3/8/17		2nd Echelon proceeded to YPRES to take over from 422nd Field Coy R.E. Orders to move next day. One M.A.H. (Inf)	RM
28 I a 3 7	4/8/17		Company moved from camp to RUE DIXMUDE, YPRES (28 I a 3.7) leaving transport en route at Wagon Lines at 28 H 2 c 0.8. One M.A.H.	RM
	5/8/17		Work started on extending tram line forward of 28 C 23 c 8.2. One M.A.H. (Inf.)	RM
	6/8/17		Work on tram line continued. Formation not drained anywhere. Existing formation to be drained, new formation to be extended, track to be laid. Ground very badly cratered, + wet. Three shell breaks	RM
	7/8/17		Line repaired, + in running order as far as old enemy front line. Three shell breaks. Two M.A.H.	RM
	8/8/17		Work on tramline continued. Repairs to Wagon track No 5 starting from Canal. One M.A.H. One reinforcement	RM
	9/8/17		As above, except that Wagon track work ceased, + mule track No 5 started forward of ~~...~~ MONMOUTH Cottage. One man evacuated, one wounded A.H., one M.A.H.	RM
	10/8/17		As above. Two men wounded. Two M.A.H., Two M.A.H. (Inf), One man evacuated.	RM

D. D. & L., London, E.C. (A7883) Wt. W203/M1672 350,000 4/17 Sch. 52a Forms/C/2118/14

Instructions regarding War Diaries and Intelligence Summaries are contained in F. S. Regs., Part II, and the Staff Manual respectively. Title pages will be prepared in manuscript.

WAR DIARY
121st Field or Company
~~INTELLIGENCE SUMMARY.~~
(Erase heading not required.)

Army Form C. 2118.

Place	Date	Hour	Summary of Events and Information	Remarks and references to Appendices
	11/8/17		As above. Work on tramline by day, on mule track by night. Spr McINTOSH killed	
			Two reinforcements. One M.A.H (Inf). One man evacuated.	RWR
	12/8/17		As above. One man wounded, two Inf: wounded, five M.A.H, three evacuated.	RWR
	13/8/17		As above. Work on wagon track started again. Lt R.E. WALSH wounded & remaining to duty	
			~~Two Inf: wounded~~ One man wounded, five M.A.H, five M.A.H (Inf:), one M.R.H.	RWR
	14/8/17		No work on tramline. Mule track completed to R. STEENBEEK. 3 bridges for Infantry	
			put across R. STEENBEEK. Wagon track made good, & marked from CANAL to MONMOUTH	
			Cottage. Four M.A.H, four evacuated, one M.A.H (Inf.)	RWR
	15/8/17		All sections resting. Marking of mule track to R. STEENBEEK completed with 6 sappers.	
			1 reinforcement, one M.A.H, one M.R.H, two evacuated, one Inf: killed.	RWR
	16/8/17		Coy in Div. Reserve. Zero hour 4.45 am. Owing to failure to reach objective, ~~[illegible]~~	
			proposed consolidation was not possible. Nothing done. One M.R.H.	RWR
	17/8/17		Sections employed by day on general improvement of No. 5 track – by night on attempted	
			~~[illegible]~~ improvement of the front line. This latter was impossible, owing to divisional relief.	
			1 Off & 100 O.R attached, rejoined their units. One M.R.H.	RWR
	18/8/17		4 Sections marched to 28 H 9 a 5 5 embussed at this point, debussed at 27 J 22 d 0.7	

D. D. & L., London, E.C.
(A7883) Wt. W803/M1672 350,000 4/17 Sch. 52a Forms/C/2118/14

Instructions regarding War Diaries and Intelligence Summaries are contained in F. S. Regs., Part II. and the Staff Manual respectively. Title pages will be prepared in manuscript.

WAR DIARY

121st Field Company

~~INTELLIGENCE SUMMARY.~~

(*Erase heading not required.*)

Army Form C. 2118.

Place	Date	Hour	Summary of Events and Information	Remarks and references to Appendices
	(cont) 18/8/17		marched to new billets along the road between 27 J 8 a 5.6 and 27 J 8 d 5 7.	
			Horse transport moved to the same billet independently by road.	RM
27 J 1 d 9.0	19/8/17		Company resting. Lieut A. FERRIER R.E & 2nd Lieut W.H. BLAGDEN attached to 150 Coy RE	
			dating 18/8/17.	RM
	20/8/17		Instructions & drill. Two reinforcements.	RM
	21/8/17		As above. Sergt MITCHELL joined. One M.A.H. Lt NORMAN proceeded to BARRASTRE as Adv.	RM
	22/8/17		As above. Orders received to move to Third Army.	RM
	23/8/17		Coy entrained at ESQUELBECQ 5.10 pm.	RM
57c O 16 d 0 9	24/8/17		Arrived BAPAUME 2.15 am. Detrained & marched to billets at 57c O 16 d 0 9.	RM
	25/8/17		Instruction & drill. 2nd Lieut DAY R.E & two sergeants proceeded to 63 Field Coy at METZ to	
			take over work.	RM
	26/8/17		Instruction & drill, 2 sections salving timber from old enemy mined dugouts near BARRASTRE	RM
	27/8/17		As above. One M.A.H, one M.R.H.	RM
METZ	28/8/17		H.Q & 4 sections marched to METZ, transport to Wagon Lines at NEUVILLE.	
			2nd Lt BLAGDEN rejoined from 150 Coy RE.	RM
	29/8/17		Work started on tunnelled dug-out at Q 10 b 9.3, & three baby elephant dugouts in the	

D. D. & L., London, E.C.
(A7883) Wt. W803/M1672 350,000 4/17 Sch. 52a. Forms/C/2118/14

Instructions regarding War Diaries and Intelligence Summaries are contained in F. S. Regs., Part II, and the Staff Manual respectively. Title pages will be prepared in manuscript.

WAR DIARY
121st Field Coy R.E.
~~INTELLIGENCE SUMMARY.~~
(*Erase heading not required.*)

Army Form C. 2118.

Place	Date	Hour	Summary of Events and Information	Remarks and references to Appendices
	(cont)			
	29/8/17		front line in Q 5 c & d. One M.A.H.	RM
	30/8/17		As above. Started erection of 2 Nissen Huts at METZ; & Battn Gum boot store at	
			Q 15 d 9.7.	RM
	31/8/17		As above.	RM
			1/9/17 R M [illegible] Maj RE	
			O.C 121st Field Coy RE	

D. D. & L., London, E.C.
(A7835) Wt. W803/M1672 350,000 4/17 Sch. 52a Forms/C/2118/14

Confidential

Vol 24

WAR DIARY

of

121st FIELD COY RE

for

MONTH of SEPTEMBER 1917.

Instructions regarding War Diaries and Intelligence Summaries are contained in F. S. Regs., Part II, and the Staff Manual respectively. Title pages will be prepared in manuscript.

WAR DIARY or INTELLIGENCE SUMMARY.

121st Field Coy R.E.

(Erase heading not required.)

Army Form C. 2118.

Place	Date	Hour	Summary of Events and Information	Remarks and references to Appendices
METZ	1/9/17		Coy distribution :- HQ & 2 & 3 Sections at METZ, 1 & 4 Sections on Det.t at Q15c 9.3, Horse lines at NEUVILLE. Work as follows :- No 1 Section constructing tunnelled dugout at Q10 b 9.3, No 4 Sect excavating & erecting 3 Baby Elephants Front Line (3' cover & 9" brick bursts), No 3 Sect erecting Rt Batt.n Gum Boot store at Q15 b 9.3 (timber tarred felt & wire netting) excavating (1st day) for Rt Batt.n Sock Drying Room at Q10d 3.9 (12' large elephant), No 2 Sect erecting Nissen Huts in METZ. 100 R/. One M.A.H. One M.R.H.	MM
	2/9/17		As above 100 R/. Part of Transport moved to METZ for daily work (4 limbers & teams)	MM
	3/9/17		As above No 2 Sect started erection of Nissens in EQUANCOURT 4 Nissens completed in METZ. Two sections resting. No R/. One reinforcement	MM
	4/9/17		As above. 3 Front Line Baby Elephants completed, 3 additional started. Two sections resting. No R/. Three platoons attached to unit for work. (10th R.I.R.). 2 evacuated.	MM
	5/9/17		As above. No 2 Sect started erection of Nissens at QrMr lines near NEUVILLE. No 3 Sect started making formation for TRESCAULT tramway extension. Both shafts of tunnelled dugout down to depth (25' cover). 50 R/. (additional to attached).	MM
	6/9/17		As above. No 4 Sect started 3 Front Line Baby Elephants. Horse lines moved from NEUVILLE to EQUANCOURT. 100 R/. Three reinforcements.	MM

D. D. & L., London, E.C. (A7883) Wt. W5o3/M1672 350,000 4/17 Sch. 52a Forms/C/2118/14

Instructions regarding War Diaries and Intelligence Summaries are contained in F. S. Regs., Part II. and the Staff Manual respectively. Title pages will be prepared in manuscript.

WAR DIARY or INTELLIGENCE SUMMARY.

121st Field Coy R.E.

(Erase heading not required.)

Army Form C. 2118.

Place	Date	Hour	Summary of Events and Information	Remarks and references to Appendices
METZ	7/9/17		As above. 130 Inf. 13 reinforcements	AWM
	8/9/17		As above. Rt Bttn Gum Boot store completed except for stove. Left ditto started at Q9d 7.8 (3 Sect)	
			2nd Lieuts M. THOMPSON R.E and J. M.C. ROBINSON R.E joined. 130 Inf. Lieut A. FERRIER R.E.	AWM
	9/9/17		As above. Two sections resting. No Inf. 1 reinforcement. [transferred to 150 Coy R.E	AWM
	10/9/17		As above. Two sections resting. No 4 Sect started 4 F.L. Baby Elephants. No Inf. One evacuated.	AWM
	11/9/17		As above. In period 4th–11th, 16 Nissens completed & 300x formation 90% complete. No 4 Sect take over latter.	
			50% completed dugout (tunnelled) at Q3b1.2 started (No 3 Sect). 180 Inf. One M.A.H.	
			2nd Lieut ROBINSON temporarily attached to 150 Coy RE	AWM
	12/9/17		As above. Sock drying room completed except for stove (4' shaft over large elephant). 180 Inf.	AWM
	13/9/17		As above. Excavation for Left Bn sock drying room started at Q3c9.4 (12' large elephant) No 3 Sect. Nissen	
			erection at Qr Mr lines completed (9 huts) 180 Inf. One M.A.H.	AWM
	14/9/17		As above. 180 Inf. Two M.A.H.	AWM
	15/9/17		All sections resting. No Inf. One man evacuated	AWM
	16/9/17		Work as usual. Low & high brushwood screen erected across road at Q8b62. No Inf.	AWM
	17/9/17		As above. No 3 Sect started 50% complete tunnelled dugout at Q3b3.2. 6 F.L. Baby Elephants completed.	
			2nd Lieut G.W.L. DAY RE transferred to 56th Field Coy RE. One man evacuated. 180 Inf.	AWM

D. D. & L., London, E.C. (A7883) Wt. W803/M1672 350,000 4/17 Sch. 52a Forms/C/2118/14

Instructions regarding War Diaries and Intelligence Summaries are contained in F. S. Regs., Part II. and the Staff Manual respectively. Title pages will be prepared in manuscript.

WAR DIARY or INTELLIGENCE SUMMARY.

121st Field Coy. R.E.

(Erase heading not required.)

Army Form C. 2118.

Place	Date	Hour	Summary of Events and Information	Remarks and references to Appendices
METZ	18/9/17		As above. In period 11th – 18th, 8 Nissens completed, & 400x formation (additional) complete 90%. 180 2/	RMM
	19/9/17		As above. 4 F.L. Baby Elephants completed. Erection of Nissen Huts at EQUANCOURT commd (6 huts) 180 2/. One evacuated.	RMM
	20/9/17		As above. Left Bn Gum Boot Store completed except for stove. Erection of Nissen Huts at METZ commd (19 huts) 2 F.L. Baby Elephants started (No 4). 180 2/. One reinforcement.	RMM
	21/9/17		All sections resting. No 2/	RMM
	22/9/17		Work as usual. A brushwood screen erected at edge of wood from Q9a04 to Q9a3.4. Three F.L. Baby Elephants started (No 4). No 2/. Concrete M.G. Dugout, in ruins at Q10b3.5 started (No 1).	RMM
	23/9/17		As above. 5 – 12' large elephants started in METZ in lieu of Nissens (No 2). 180 2/.	RMM
	24/9/17		As above. Left Battn Sock drying room complete except for stove. 180 2/	RMM
	25/9/17		As above. 5 F.L. Baby Elephants completed. In period 18th – 25th, 6 Nissens & 1100 yards formation completed. Excavation complete of tunnelled dugouts at Q3b3.2 & Q3b1.2. 2nd Lieut NORMAN R.E. detached to ROCQUIGNY under C.R.E.'s orders. 180 2/.	RMM
	26/9/17		As above. Second brushwood screen erected at edge of wood from Q9a04 to Q9a34. (No 3). Excavation started for concrete Coy H.Q. dugout at Q4a1.1 (No 3). 180 2/. Sapper WALLIS wounded by H.E. and A.H. One man evacuated. One M.A.H.	RMM

D. D. & L., London, E.C. (A7883) Wt. W803/M1672 350,000 4/17 Sch. 52a Forms/C/2118/14

Instructions regarding War Diaries and Intelligence Summaries are contained in F. S. Regs., Part II. and the Staff Manual respectively. Title pages will be prepared in manuscript.

Army Form C. 2118.

WAR DIARY or ~~INTELLIGENCE SUMMARY.~~

121st Field Coy R.E.

(Erase heading not required.)

Place	Date	Hour	Summary of Events and Information	Remarks and references to Appendices
METZ	27/9/17		All sections resting. No Inf	RM
	28/9/17		Work as usual. No Inf 6 F.L. Baby Elephants started (2 & 3). Concrete M.G. Dugout started at Q 9 a 2.9 (No 3). Work of all 4 sections readjusted. No 1 Sect absorbed by replacing other section sappers on various detachments. No 2 moved forward to replace No 4 in advanced billet – No 4 to H.Q. No 3 doing all forward work left of TRESCAULT stream, No 2 right of stream, No 4 back area work on Bde front. One M.A.H. One M.R.H. One man wounded.	RM
	29/9/17		As above. No 4 Sect started installation of 6 Spray BAIN DOUCHE in METZ baths. 1802 [illegible]	RM
	30/9/17		As above. Last day of work of Attd 3 Platoons – ordered to rejoin Battn 1/10/17.	RM
			N.B. M.A.H. Men Admitted to Hospital. M.R.H. Men Rejoined from Hospital.	
			Remarks. Owing to personnel required for Div. work hutting, dumps, etc – and construction of stables for the unit, average strength of sappers employed on [illegible] for the whole month, was 75 daily.	
			1/10/17. [signature] Maj RE O.C. 121st Field Coy RE	

D. D. & L., London, E.C. (A7883) Wt. W593/M1672 350,000 4/17 Sch. 52a Forms/C/2118/14

Confidential

Vol 25

War Diary

of

121st Field Coy RE

for

Month of October 1917

Instructions regarding War Diaries and Intelligence Summaries are contained in F. S. Regs., Part II. and the Staff Manual respectively. Title pages will be prepared in manuscript.

WAR DIARY
121st Field Coy R.E.
INTELLIGENCE SUMMARY.

(Erase heading not required.)

Army Form C. 2118.

Place	Date	Hour	Summary of Events and Information	Remarks and references to Appendices
	1/10/17		Coy distribution H.Q. and 3 & 4 Sections at METZ, 2 Section on Det at Q 15 C 9.3 No 1 Section split up, part at ROCQUIGNY working on reinforcement camp and part at YTRES working on new Divisional H.Q. Horse lines at EQUANCOURT. 18 animals at METZ Work as follows in addition to above:- Deep dugouts at Q 10 b 9.3 and Q 11 C 5.1 Front line Baby Elephant dugouts Two in B Sap, Two in C Sap, Two in E Sap, one in D Sap, one at front line end of D Sap, ~~and~~ three in front line and four at junction of A Sap & front line. Six large elephants being erected in cellars in METZ, sock drying rooms at Q 10 d 3.9 and Q 3 a 9.4. FRESCAULT Tramway being extended	Ml
	2/10/17		Work as above. Working parties 220.	Ml
	3/10/17		Rest day owing to relief	Ml
	4/10/17		Work as above working parties 220.	Ml.
	5/10/17		Work as above. Two Baby Elephants in E Sap Completed. 1 M.A.H.	Ml
	6/10/17		Work as above four Baby Elephants at junction of A Sap & Front line completed 1 M.D.H.	Ml
	7/10/17		Work as above Two Sock drying rooms completed.	Ml.
	8/10/17		Work as above 1 M.D.H.	Ml.
	9/10/17		Rest day owing to relief. Major Lewin proceeded on one months leave.	Ml.

Instructions regarding War Diaries and Intelligence Summaries are contained in F. S. Regs., Part II, and the Staff Manual respectively. Title pages will be prepared in manuscript.

WAR DIARY
121st Field Coy.
INTELLIGENCE SUMMARY.
(Erase heading not required.)

Army Form C. 2118.

Place	Date	Hour	Summary of Events and Information	Remarks and references to Appendices
	10/10/17		Work as above Working Parties 60 men Total 1 Man Evacuated.	H.G.
	11/10/17		" " " " 220 men Total 1 M.A.H.	H.G.
	12/10/17		" " Two Baby Elephants in B Sap Completed	H.G.
			One " " for Rt Battn R.A.P Commenced	
	13/10/17		" " Two Baby Elephants in C Sap Completed. 3 Reinforcements joined Coy.	H.G.
			Three " " Commenced in Inscault Trench 2.M.A.H.	
			Three " " " " Fusiliers Post	
			Scrummy Sap in wood at Q15C28. Commenced.	H.G.
	14/10/17		Tunnelled Dugout Mcty Q19a5.4 Commenced. other work as above. 2 MAH.	H.G.
	15/10/17		Rest day owing to relief. attached Infy rejoined	H.G.
	16/10/17		Work as above. No working parties. 3 men taking ammonal torpedoes.	H.G.
	17/10/17		" " " Working Parties 140 men. 2 men sent to divisional dump	H.G.
			70 men of 8th/9th R.I.R. attached	
	18/10/17		Work as above. Commenced erecting Englesh Shelters at EQUANCOURT. Working Parties 200 men.	H.G.
			Cross country Track M125 2 to YTRES Started.	
	19/10/17		Improvements to Entrances of Centre Coy & Left Coy of left Battalion Commenced. 4 reinforcements arrived 2 M.A.H	H.G.

D. D. & L., London, E.C. (A7883) Wt. W593/M1672 350,000 4/17 Sch. 52a. Forms/C/2118/14

Instructions regarding War Diaries and Intelligence Summaries are contained in F. S. Regs., Part II, and the Staff Manual respectively. Title pages will be prepared in manuscript.

Army Form C. 2118.

WAR DIARY
121st Field Coy R.E.
INTELLIGENCE SUMMARY.
(*Erase heading not required.*)

Place	Date	Hour	Summary of Events and Information	Remarks and references to Appendices
	20/10/17		Work as above. Elephants in METZ Completed. One baby Elephant at R.T. Batter RAP Completed	H.L.
	21/10/17		Rest day.	H.L.
	22/10/17		Working Parties 60. Work as above. Baby Elephants in Bays 78 & 82 Completed.	H.L.
	23/10/17		Working Parties 220. Work as above. Commenced making movable targets for rifle range. 1 M.D.H.	H.L.
	24/10/17		Work as above. Screening of Gap in Wood completed. 1 Man wounded, remains at duty.	H.L.
	25/10/17		Two baby Elephants in B Sap completed. Screening of TUFNELL AVENUE Commenced. 1 M.D.H.	H.L.
	26/10/17		One " " C " " Two men wounded remain at duty.	H.L.
	27/10/17		One " " A " " . Rest Day for rest of company.	H.L.
	28/10/17		One " " Bay 93 Completed Working Parties total 60 men. Erection of two Elephants in TRESCAULT Station,	
			Repair of road from METZ to A.D.S. Commenced. Erection of English shelters in EQUANCOURT Commenced	H.L.
	29/10/17		Tunnelled dugout at No 1 Post Completed. 1 M.A.H.	
			Two sections of 457th Field Coy attached for work on METZ – TRESCAULT Road.	
			Four Nissen Huts at EQUANCOURT Transport lines Completed except for lining.	H.L.
	30/10/17		Work as above. Targets for rifle range completed.	
			Erection of Warming Room for men of Coy in METZ Started	H.L.
	31/10/17		Work as above.	H.L.

121st COY. ROYAL ENGINEERS No. S 707 Date 31/10/17 ULSTER DIVISION

H. Lucock Capt R.E.
O.C. 121 Field Coy R.E.

D. D. & L., London, E.C. (A7883) Wt. W803/M1672 350,000 4/17 Sch. 52a Forms/C/2118/14

Confidential

Vol 26

WAR DIARY

of

121st Field Company R.E.

for month of NOVEMBER, 1917

SECRET

Army Form C. 2118.

Instructions regarding War Diaries and Intelligence Summaries are contained in F. S. Regs., Part II, and the Staff Manual respectively. Title pages will be prepared in manuscript.

WAR DIARY
121st Field Coy RE
~~INTELLIGENCE SUMMARY.~~
(Erase heading not required.)

M.A.H. Man admitted to hospital
M.R.H. Man rejoined from hospital

Place	Date	Hour	Summary of Events and Information	Remarks and references to Appendices
METZ	1/11/17		HQ & 3 & 4 Sections at METZ, 2 Section in HAVRINCOURT WOOD (Q 15 d 4.2), 1 Section dispersed in detachments, Horse lines at EQUANCOURT. Company working at tunnelled dugouts at Q11 c 5.1, Q4 a 15.10, Q11 b 8.8; concrete dugouts for M.G. crews at Q10 b 3.5, Q9 a 2.9; erecting 2 large elephants in TRESCAULT, Baby Elephants in the Front Line & supports; screening METZ-TRESCAULT road, TUFFNELL AV; making new road to ADS; making warming room at METZ. 200 Inf.	RWM
	2/11/17		Rest day for all sections	RWM
	3/11/17		Work as above. One large elephant at TRESCAULT completed. 200 Inf.	RWM
	4/11/17		As above. Spr Rothwell killed by H.E. 200 Inf.	RWM
	5/11/17		As above. Horse lines moved to LECHELLE. One M.A.H.	RWM
	6/11/17		As above. 6 Front line elephants completed in preceding week. 200 Inf.	RWM
	7/11/17		As above. 2 men evacuated. Spr Green wounded and admitted hospital. 160 Inf.	RWM
	8/11/17		As above. One M.R.H. Work on all Front Line Baby Elephants suspended by order of C.R.E. 160 Inf.	RWM
	9/11/17		As above. One M.A.H. All screening completed. 160 Inf.	RWM
	10/11/17		As above. Large elephant at TRESCAULT completed. 160 Inf. One M.A.H.	RWM
	11/11/17		As above. Tunnelled dugout at Q4 a 15.10 completed. 160 Inf.	RWM
	12/11/17		As above. Tunnelled dugout at Q11 b 8.8 handed over to N.Z. Tunnelling Coy. One M.R.H. 160 Inf.	RWM

D. D. & L., London, E.C.
(A7883) Wt. W593/M1672 350,000 4/17 Sch. 52a Forms/C/2118/14

SECRET

Army Form C. 2118.

WAR DIARY
121st Field Coy RE
~~INTELLIGENCE SUMMARY.~~
(Erase heading not required.)

Instructions regarding War Diaries and Intelligence Summaries are contained in F. S. Regs., Part II. and the Staff Manual respectively. Title pages will be prepared in manuscript.

Place	Date	Hour	Summary of Events and Information	Remarks and references to Appendices
METZ	13/11/17		As above. Road to A.D.S completed. Two M.R.H, one evacuated. 120 2/f.	RM
	14/11/17		Concrete dugout at Q10b 3.5 completed. All other work in the line suspended by order. Company concentrated on road work, and ~~transport~~ of road material & trench boards to TRESCAULT.	
			Sgt Preston evacuated. 120 2/f.	RM
	15/11/17		Road work as above; on METZ – TRESCAULT road by night, and METZ – PLACE MONTMARDE road by day.	RM
	16/11/17		Road work as above.	RM
	17/11/17		As above. 2 officers and 100 OR Infantry attached for work. Horse lines to YTRES	RM
	18/11/17		As above. One M.R.H. one evacuated.	
HAVRINCOURT WOOD	19/11/17		HQ & remaining 3 sections moved to HAVRINCOURT WOOD Q15d 4 2. Road work ceased.	
			No 3 Section filled in Spt line crossing, & bridged Front line crossing of TRESCAULT – RIBECOURT road during night 19/20.	RM
	20/11/17		Zero hour 6.20 am. No 2 Section moved at 9.20 am, & worked at [illegible] of Front line & Spt line crossings. Nos 1 & 4 Sections moved at am, and under instructions of O.C. [illegible] RE cleared the road of tram lines & other obstacles between L 25 c 0 2 and L 25 d 3.2. These sections were relieved at 4.0 pm by No 3 Section, which carried on with work at craters at K 36 c 0 0, & transport of material for this, from TRESCAULT railhead. Attached Inf: worked with the [illegible] sections.	RM

D. D. & L., London, E.C. (A7883) Wt. W803/M1672 350,000 4/17 Sch. 52a Forms/C/2118/14

SECRET

Army Form C. 2118.

Instructions regarding War Diaries and Intelligence Summaries are contained in F. S. Regs., Part II. and the Staff Manual respectively. Title pages will be prepared in manuscript.

WAR DIARY
121st Field Coy RE
~~INTELLIGENCE SUMMARY.~~
(*Erase heading not required.*)

Place	Date	Hour	Summary of Events and Information	Remarks and references to Appendices
HAVRINCOURT WOOD	21/11/17		Nos 1, 2, 4 Sections worked in 2 – 6 hour shifts at the corduroy diversion round crater at K 36 c 0 0. No 3 Section worked night transport of stores, which owing to the congestion of the roads was unusually low.	AM
	22/11/17		As above. Corduroy diversion completed before dark. Orders received to cease all work.	AM
HERMIES	23/11/17		HQ & 4 Sections moved to a tent camp at HERMIES J 30 c 5.7. No work done.	AM
	24/11/17		Coy employed on repair & clearing of road from J 18 d 35 to J 13 b 4.8	AM
	25/11/17		No 1 Sect & 25 Inf. moved to dugouts at E 29 a 0 6, & cmd front line in E 23 c. Remaining sections on road clearing as above. Cor M.A.H.	AM
	26/11/17		No 1 Section as above. Nos 2, 3, 4 wiring reserve line in E 28 b. & reinforcements	AM
	27/11/17		No 1 Section and Inf. rejoined. No night work, sections 12 hours rest.	AM
	28/11/17		Nos 1 & 4 Sections started corduroy road at K 14 a 3.1 at side of track running N.E. Nos 2 & 3 started erection of elephants in HERMIES, as a Coy billet. Orders received at 3.0 pm to move by train & road the next day	AM
GOMIECOURT	29/11/17		HQ & transport marched to GOMIECOURT via BERTINCOURT, HAPLINCOURT, BAPAUME, BIHUCOURT, & camped there. 4 Sections marched to YTRES Station entrained, & detrained at BEAUMETZ Station, marched to BERNEVILLE & into billets. (2.0 am 30/11/17)	AM

D. D. & L., London, E.C.
(A7883) Wt. W803/M1672 350,000 4/17 Sch. 52a. Forms/C/2118/14

SECRET

Army Form C. 2118.

Instructions regarding War Diaries and Intelligence Summaries are contained in F. S. Regs., Part II. and the Staff Manual respectively. Title pages will be prepared in manuscript.

WAR DIARY

121st Field Coy RE

~~INTELLIGENCE SUMMARY.~~

(*Erase heading not required.*)

Place	Date	Hour	Summary of Events and Information	Remarks and references to Appendices
COURCELLES	30/4/17		HQ & transport reached BEAUMETZ ~~at~~ en route for BERNEVILLE going via COURCELLES, AYETTE, RANSART when orders were received to march to billets at COURCELLES, and returned by the same route. 4 Sections marched from BERNEVILLE to COURCELLES via WAILLY, FICHEUX, BOIRY, AYETTE. arriving ~~at~~ at billets at midnight.	RM

11/12/17

R M [illegible] Major RE
O.C. 121st Field Coy RE

D. D. & L., London, E.C. (A7883) Wt. W803/M1672 350,000 1/17 Sch. 52a Forms/C/2118/14

SECRET

Vol 27

War Diary

of

121st Field Coy RE

for

December 1917

WAR DIARY
or
~~INTELLIGENCE SUMMARY.~~
(*Erase heading not required.*)

Army Form C. 2118.

Instructions regarding War Diaries and Intelligence Summaries are contained in F. S. Regs., Part II, and the Staff Manual respectively. Title pages will be prepared in manuscript.

M.A.H. Man admitted to hospital
M.R.H " rejoined from "

Place	Date	Hour	Summary of Events and Information	Remarks and references to Appendices
BEAULENCOURT	1/12/17		Unit moved from COURCELLES to BEAULENCOURT (Staging Area). Start 2.30pm, arrived 6 pm.	
			5 M.A.H. Att^d Inf: rejoined their respective Battns.	AML
LECHELLE	2/12/17		March continued (10.30am) to LECHELLE (1.30pm). Two M.A.H.	AML
	3/12/17		Unit resting. Two M.A.H	AML
DESSART WOOD	4/12/17		No 3 Section marched to billets at METZ, transport to billets at SOREL-LE-GRAND, remainder to bivouac at DESSART WOOD. No 4 Sect then joined No 3 Sect at METZ. Two M.A.H.	AML
METZ	5/12/17		No 3 Sect started conversion of deep dug-out at Q25c99 into Hdqrs for Div: Nos 1 & 2 Sects and H.Q proceeded to METZ. 1 man evacuated.	AML
	6/12/17		3 Sect as above, remainder wiring by night, a new Reserve Line from R7b3.6 through R1d8.1 to R2c5.2. Three M.R.H. 6 men evacuated.	AML
	7/12/17		As above. 200 Inf: 1 man evacuated.	AML
	8/12/17		As above, except No 2 Sect resting. 400 Inf: Four M.A.H	AML
	9/12/17		No 3 Sect as before, Nos 1 & 4 resting. Wiring of Reserve Line handed over to 150 Coy RE. No 2 Sect in three parties formed part of 3 bombing parties, to establish Trench blocks in trenches at R10c 20.65, R10c 20.95, R10a 60.73. The first was successful, the other two failed, & no R.E. work was possible. No Inf. 4 M.A.H.	AML

Map Reference from Sheet 57c 1/40,000 series AML

D. D. & L., London, E.C. (A7883) Wt. W803/M1672 350,000 4/17 Sch. 52a Forms/C/2118/14

Army Form C. 2118.

WAR DIARY
or
~~INTELLIGENCE SUMMARY.~~
(Erase heading not required.)

Instructions regarding War Diaries and Intelligence Summaries are contained in F. S. Regs., Part II, and the Staff Manual respectively. Title pages will be prepared in manuscript.

Maps 57 C until 14/12/17
Lens 11 after 14/12/17

Place	Date	Hour	Summary of Events and Information	Remarks and references to Appendices
METZ	10/12/17		No 2 Sect moved to forward billets at R 3 C 10 . 80 + started wiring of Front Line from R 4 C 7 . 5 working westwards. 100 Inf. No 3 + 4 Sects on Div H.Q. No 1 resting. 1 killed + 3 wounded by H.E. in billet at METZ, and admitted hospital. 3 M.A.H.	A.M.
	11/12/17		3 + 4 Sections as above. No 1 + 2 wiring as above. No 1 Sect moved to join No 2. Two evacuated One M.A.H. 2nd Lt THOMPSON R.E. admitted to hospital. 100 Inf.	A.M.
	12/12/17		Work as above 100 Inf. Two M.A.H. 6 evacuated 3 reinforcements	A.M.
	13/12/17		Work as above. Three M.A.H. One M.R.H. 25 Inf.	A.M.
	14/12/17		All work handed over to 62nd Div RE. 1 + 2 Sects rejoined H.Q.	A.M.
MANANCOURT	15/12/17		Unit marched to MANANCOURT, into tents.	A.M.
	16/12/17		Unit resting + cleaning. Two men evacuated. Two M.R.H. 1 reinforcement. Heavy fall of snow at night.	A.M.
BEAUDRICOURT	17/12/17		Transport less 3 limbers marched to COURCELLES. Remainder entrained ETRICOURT detrained MONDICOURT marched to BEAUDRICOURT into rest billets at 9.0 pm.	A.M.
	18/12/17		Transport compelled to leave 4 Tool carts + 2 Pontoon wagons at L'ESPERANCE owing to exhaustion of horses with the snow. — arrived BEAUDRICOURT 3.0 am 19/12/17.	A.M.
	19/12/17		All sections clearing roads of snow	A.M.
	20/12/17		Abandoned transport of 18/12/17 brought in. Road clearing as above. Two M.R.H.	A.M.

D. D. & L., London, E.C. (A7883) Wt. W803/M1672 350,000 4/17 Sch. 52a Forms/C/2118/14

Instructions regarding War Diaries and Intelligence Summaries are contained in F. S. Regs., Part II. and the Staff Manual respectively. Title pages will be prepared in manuscript.

WAR DIARY

or

~~INTELLIGENCE SUMMARY.~~

(*Erase heading not required.*)

Army Form C. 2118.

Maps Lens 11 Amiens

Place	Date	Hour	Summary of Events and Information	Remarks and references to Appendices
BEAUDRICOURT	21/12/17		Road clearing as before. Unit responsible for BEAUDRICOURT – SUS ST LEGER road.	
			2nd Lt ROBINSON R E attached to C E V. Corps	AM
	22/12/17		Road clearing as above. Three M.A.H. Two M.R.H	AM
	23/12/17		Road clearing as above. One M.R.H	AM
	24/12/17		As above.	AM
	25/12/17		Christmas day. General holiday.	AM
	26/12/17		Transport less Tool Cart wagon and 4 limbers marched to PUCHEVILLERS. Three M.A.H.	AM
WAREUSEE –	27/12/17		Remainder of unit marched at 5.0 am, entrained at MONDICOURT, detrained at CORBIE, marched to	
ABANCOURT			WAREUSEE – ABANCOURT into rest billets. Transport arrived 11.50 pm	AM
	28/12/17		Training & drill. One M.A.H.	AM
	29/12/17		As above. 2nd Lt POTTS RE joined unit to replace 2nd Lt THOMPSON. R.E.	AM
	30/12/17		As above	AM
	31/12/17		As above.	AM

A McLeroin Maj RE

O.C. 121st Field Coy RE

1/1/18

D. D. & L., London, E.C. (A7883) Wt. W8o7/M1672 350,000 4/17 Sch. 52a Forms/C/2118/14

Confidential

Vol 28

War Diary

— of —

121st Field Coy. R.E.

for Jany. 1918

Instructions regarding War Diaries and Intelligence Summaries are contained in F. S. Regs., Part II. and the Staff Manual respectively. Title pages will be prepared in manuscript.

WAR DIARY
or
~~INTELLIGENCE SUMMARY.~~
(Erase heading not required.)

Maps
Sheets 17, 18 – 1/100,000
Sheet 66 D – 1/40,000

Army Form C. 2118.

M.A.H. Man admitted to hospital
M.R.H. Man rejoined from hospital

Place	Date	Hour	Summary of Events and Information	Remarks and references to Appendices
WARFUSEE ABANCOURT	1/1/18		Unit in rest billets. Training and drill	ARM
	2/1/18		As above. Lt WALSH to U.K on leave.	ARM
	3/1/18		As above. One M.R.H	ARM
	4/1/18		As above 1 Man evacuated	ARM
	5/1/18		As above. 4 reinforcements	ARM
	6/1/18		As above. Advanced billeting officer sent to FRAMERVILLE.	ARM
FRAMERVILLE	7/1/18		Unit marched to FRAMERVILLE. – arriving 1.0 pm. 1 Man evacuated	ARM
	8/1/18		Training and drill. Advanced billeting officer sent to VOYENNES	ARM
VOYENNES	9/1/18		Unit marched to VOYENNES arriving 4.0 pm.	ARM
	10/1/18		Cleaning harness, washing wagons. Lt BLAGDEN and Sergt MC ROBERTS ~~proceed~~ proceeded to 1/3rd Company of Engineers, Greek Army, at HAMEL to take over work.	ARM
DURY	11/1/18		Unit marched to DURY, billets at OLLEZY (the original destination) being unavailable. 4 reinforcements	ARM
	12/1/18		Cleaning harness, washing wagons, boat rehearsal drill. 6 M.A.H.	ARM
	13/1/18		Three sections marched to advanced billets of 1/3rd Company of Engineers at 66 d F.18 a 7.4. Lt PITTS to AIRE for Bridging Course. Three M.A.H. 5 reinforcements.	ARM

A5834 Wt. W4973/M687 750,000 8/16 D. D. & L. Ltd. Forms/C.2118/13.

Instructions regarding War Diaries and Intelligence Summaries are contained in F. S. Regs., Part II. and the Staff Manual respectively. Title pages will be prepared in manuscript.

WAR DIARY
or
~~INTELLIGENCE SUMMARY.~~
(Erase heading not required.)

Army Form C. 2118.

Sheets 62 C SE, 62 B SW, 66 D NE, 66 C NW.

Place	Date	Hour	Summary of Events and Information	Remarks and references to Appendices
HAMEL	14/1/18		H.Q. & transport ~~[illegible]~~ marched to HAMEL – taking over from 1/3rd Company. Gen M.R.H.	R.M.
	15/1/18		Cleaning & improvement of billets	R.M.
	16/1/18		~~[illegible]~~ Excavation started for new Bn HQ at A 9 a 0.4 ; wiring intermediate line in F 12 C started; repairs to bridges between HAMEL and GRAND SERAUCOURT taken in hand. 2 reinforcements	R.M.
	17/1/18		As above. A hut for Rt Bn H.Q. started at A 18 b 37., and for one for R.A.P. started at A 18 b 5.7 ; a new gum boot drying room started at G 28 b 33 ; Bn HQ at A 9 a 0 4 cancelled, work ceased. Gen M.R.H	R.M.
	18/1/18		As above. Erection of a dugout for a Bde Visual Station started at A 4 c 0.8. Started new O.P. at S 21 b 23 Gen M.R.H.	R.M.
	19/1/18		As above. Excavation for new Battn HQ started at A 15 d 0 7. 2 men transferred to 122 Coy RE. Lt WALSH to U.K on leave.	R.M.
	20/1/18		As above. 4 men evacuated. 1 M.R.H.	R.M.
	21/1/18		As above. Screening repairs started at A 11 a. 1 man evacuated. Gen M.R.H.	R.M.
	22/1/18		As above. Screening repairs completed. New Battn H.Q. cancelled, work ceased. Making causeway across marsh in A 21 c taken over from 150 Coy RE. Gen M.R.H.	R.M.
	23/1/18		As above. Wiring Bn/Bde line handed over to XVIII Corps – 1300x double apron fence erected. Repairs to HAMEL bridges completed. Improvement to A.D.S. at A 3 d 54 started. Conversion of work house at A 18 d 66 into bath house for 3rd Battn started. Capt GOOCH to U K on leave.	R.M.

A5834 Wt. W4973/M687 750,000 8/16 D. D. & L. Ltd. Forms/C.2118/13.

Instructions regarding War Diaries and Intelligence Summaries are contained in F. S. Regs., Part II. and the Staff Manual respectively. Title pages will be prepared in manuscript.

WAR DIARY
or
~~INTELLIGENCE SUMMARY.~~
(Erase heading not required.)

Army Form C. 2118.

Place	Date	Hour	Summary of Events and Information	Remarks and references to Appendices
HAMEL	24/1/18		Rest day. Inspection & drill. 8 reinforcements. 1 M.R.H.	RWM
	25/1/18		Work as usual. Making new advanced billets at GIFFECOURT started (A11c6.4). One M.A.H.	RWM
	26/1/18		As above. O.P. at S21 b 2.3 completed – consists of a [illegible] [illegible], & [illegible] box 6'x3' sunk 6' into the ground. Wiring NOUVELLE TRENCH in S22 d started (wooden [illegible]). One M.A.H. One man evacuated.	RWM
	27/1/18		As above. One M.A.H. One man evacuated.	RWM
	28/1/18		As above. Dugout at Bde O.P. completed at A4c0.8 – consists of 6' elephant [illegible] a brick wall with a rectangular entrance 6'x6', two walls of which have long slit loopholes for observation. No. 4 Section [illegible] at disposal of 122 Coy RE for work with Div. artillery in 107 Bde area. Two M.R.H., 3 evacuated.	RWM
	29/1/18		As above. Hut at 13b3.7 completed ([illegible] & C.G.I. sides [illegible] [illegible] roof). [illegible] [illegible] [illegible] completed (brick floor laid with cement [illegible]). One M.A.H.	RWM
	30/1/18		Rest day. Inspection & drill. Lt POTTS rejoined from Bridging Course	RWM
	31/1/18		~~As above~~ Work as usual. Placing substructure on bridge left by the French uncompleted at A26c2.5, started. One man evacuated.	RWM

R W [illegible] Maj RE
O.C. 121st Field Coy RE
1/2/18

A5834 Wt. W4973/M687 750,000 8/16 D. D. & L. Ltd. Forms/C.2118/13.

VR 29

Confidential

War Diary

of

O.C. 121st Field Coy R.E.

for month of February 1918

Instructions regarding War Diaries and Intelligence Summaries are contained in F. S. Regs., Part II. and the Staff Manual respectively. Title pages will be prepared in manuscript.

WAR DIARY
or
INTELLIGENCE SUMMARY.
(Erase heading not required.)

121 Field Coy R.E.

Army Form C. 2118.

Place	Date	Hour	Summary of Events and Information	Remarks and references to Appendices
1-2-18	1/2/18		Work consisted of 1 Section wiring front line left subsector. 1 Section making forward billets at GIFFECOURT. 1 Section working on mined dugouts for R.A. & 1 Section at H.Q. working on Causeway at A21C, making latrine boards, repairing entrances of mined dugouts, constructing [illegible] drying room at left batt. HQ & repairing A.D.S. & constructing R.A.P. for right battn. one MAH.	H.S.
	2/2/18		Work as above. 1 MAH.	H.S.
	3/2/18		" " " Screening DALLON - GRUGIES Track commenced.	H.S.
	4/2/18		" " " Bath house at DALLON started. Wiring support line at battalion started.	H.S.
			Cpl King awarded Croix de Guerre.	
	5/2/18		Rest Day	H.S.
	6/2/18		1 Reinforcement joined coy. Pontoon bridge erected at FONTAIN-LES-CLERCS.	
	7/2/18		6 " " " 1 MAH 1 Man wounded.	H.S.
	8/2/18		Wiring of front line ceased. Dugout for 1 Platoon started at GIFFECOURT. Superstructure of bridge at A26C2.4 started.	H.S.
	9/2/18		1 Reinforcement joined coy.	
	10/2/18		1 MDH.	H.S.
	11/2/18		Dugout for 1 platoon at GIFFECOURT completed. Wiring front line left sector started.	H.S.
	12/2/18		1 MAH. Bridge at A26C2.4 completed. RAP for right battalion completed.	H.S.
	13/2/18		Work as above.	H.S.
	14/2/18		" " " 2 MAH.	H.S.
	15/2/18		REST DAY	H.S.
	16/2/18		1 Man evacuated. No 1 Section moved to H.Q. Work started on L'ERMITE de DALLON	H.S.
	17/2/18		1 MDH. Work commenced on tunnelled dugout in quarry at L6C	H.S.

A5834 Wt. W4973/M687 750,000 8/16 D. D. & L. Ltd. Forms/C.2118/13.

Instructions regarding War Diaries and Intelligence Summaries are contained in F. S. Regs., Part II. and the Staff Manual respectively. Title pages will be prepared in manuscript.

WAR DIARY
or
INTELLIGENCE SUMMARY.
(Erase heading not required.)

12th Field Coy R.E.

Army Form C. 2118.

Place	Date	Hour	Summary of Events and Information	Remarks and references to Appendices
	18/2/18		Work started on S.P. at A17 central.	H.G.
	19/2/18		Work as above. 1 M.D.H.	H.G.
	20/2/18		Took over work in Battle Zone south of Canal, consisting of construction of series of strongpoints, keeps & redoubts, from 201st Field Coy R.E. No 2 Section moved from forward billets to H.Q.	H.G.
	21/2/18		Sixteen reinforcements joined Coy.	H.G.
	22/2/18		3 M.A.H.	
	23/2/18		2/Lt D. WEIGHTON joined Coy from 238 A.T. Coy. Work in Battle Zone north of Canal taken over from 202nd Field Coy. Work on two New Bn H.Q. handed over to 750th Field Coy R.E. 3 Sections on the Battle Zone. 1 Section still employed with R.A. building O.Ps.	H.G.
	24/2/18		1 Man evacuated.	
	25/2/18		Work as above. 1 Man evacuated.	
	26/2/18		2 Reinforcements joined Coy.	H.G.
	27/2/18		Work as above.	H.G.
	28/2/18		Work as above.	H.G.
				H.G.
				H.G.

H. Hood Capt R.E.
O.C. 12 Field Coy R.E.

A5834 Wt. W4973/M687 750,000 8/16 D. D. & L. Ltd. Forms/C.2118/13.

Secret

36

Vol 30

War Diary

of

121st Field Company R E

for month of March 1918

Instructions regarding War Diaries and Intelligence Summaries are contained in F. S. Regs., Part II. and the Staff Manual respectively. Title pages will be prepared in manuscript.

WAR DIARY 121st Field Coy R.E.
or
~~INTELLIGENCE SUMMARY.~~
(*Erase heading not required.*)

Army Form C. 2118.

Place	Date	Hour	Summary of Events and Information	Remarks and references to Appendices
LE HAMEL	1/3/18		Sections 1, 2 & 3 Employed on Battle Zone. Section 4 Employed with R. Artillery. Battle Zone work consists of construction of Redoubts Keeps and Strong Points and connecting them up by communication trenches. Men were employed on wiring; Erection of Baby Elephant Shelters in the Trenches in Battle Zone, Ammunition and Ration recesses. No 4 Section work consisted chiefly of construction of O.Ps. Total working party strength about 700	HG
	2/3/18		Work as above	HG
	3/3/18		do	HG
	4/3/18		do one man evacuated to C.C.S. Working Party strength 600	HG
	5/3/18		do	HG
	6/3/18		do	HG
	7/3/18		do Two men admitted to Hospital Working Party strength 500	HG
	8/3/18		do	HG
	9/3/18		do one man evacuated 3 men admitted to Hospital.	HG
	10/3/18		do	HG
	11/3/18		do	HG
	12/3/18		do Demolition of five bridges over canal and river close to LE HAMEL rehearsed.	HG
	13/3/18		do 5 men for dental treatment.	HG
	14/3/18		do	HG
	15/3/18		do	HG

A5834 Wt. W4973/M687 750,000 8/16 D. D. & L. Ltd. Forms/C.2118/13.

Instructions regarding War Diaries and Intelligence Summaries are contained in F. S. Regs., Part II. and the Staff Manual respectively. Title pages will be prepared in manuscript.

WAR DIARY
or
~~INTELLIGENCE SUMMARY~~.
(Erase heading not required.)

121st Field Coy R.E.

Army Form C. 2118.

Place	Date	Hour	Summary of Events and Information	Remarks and references to Appendices
	16/3/18		Work on battle zone and with R.F.A as above. 2 Men Transferred from 122 Field Coy R.E.	JHG
	17/3/18		ST. PATRICKS DAY. A holiday for whole Coy. 1 Reinforcement arrived.	JHG
	18/3/18		Work as on 16th.	JHG
	19/3/18		" " above	JHG
	20/3/18		" " " . Received warning of impending enemy attacks.	JHG
	21/3/18		Heavy hostile bombardment commenced between 4 AM and 5.10 AM. ~~Received~~	
		5.30 AM	Received order "Man battle stations". No 1 Section under 2/Lt NORMAN R.E. immediately prepared all bridges in the HAMEL – SERAUCOURT group for demolition as previously arranged, and stood by for orders. All wagons were packed and horse lines and Transport ^Section cooks^ ~~was~~ moved to site previously selected near TUGNY. Rest of Coy stood by for orders at billets at LE-HAMEL	
		3.0 PM	Received orders by Telephone to move Nos 2, 3 and 4 sections back to Horse Lines near TUGNY. No 1 Section remained for bridge demolition.	
		12.10 PM	Pontoon bridge and footbridge at FONTAINE-LES-CLERCS demolished completely having been previously rendered unserviceable by direct hits. There was very heavy shelling in this area. Sheet 66 C NW A15 d 3.7.	
		10.15 PM	Bridge No 40 ~~at~~ and the footbridge over Canal ^north of^ ~~opposite~~ LE-HAMEL Sucrerie were demolished at 10.15 PM under orders received from Infantry occupying sector close by. This bridge had been heavily shelled and the leads to the explosives had been cut three times. 2/Cpl Rainbird did very good work here. Map reference of bridge Sheet 66 C NW A 26 c 1.2.	JHG
		11.45 PM	Bridges 35A and 35B demolished by Cpl BURSTON under orders of officer of 107 Infy Bde after all their men had crossed. Orders were received from 108th Infy Bde ~~not~~ to delay this demolition until their men had crossed but the orders arrived just too late. It was not known that 108 Bde would use this bridge in their retirement. Map Refce of bridge Sheet 66 C NW G 2 c 4.4. Horse lines were moved to PITHON arriving about 1.0 AM 22/3/18	
	22.3.18.	2.0 AM	2/Lt BLAGDEN and 1 Sapper were sent off on bicycles to blow up an ammunition dump but found that all the ammunition had been removed	JHG

Instructions regarding War Diaries and Intelligence Summaries are contained in F. S. Regs., Part II. and the Staff Manual respectively. Title pages will be prepared in manuscript.

WAR DIARY
or
~~INTELLIGENCE SUMMARY.~~
(Erase heading not required.)

121st Field Coy R.E.

Army Form C. 2118.

Place	Date	Hour	Summary of Events and Information	Remarks and references to Appendices
	22.3.18	3.0 AM.	Bridge 34A viz main bridge over Canal connecting LE-HAMEL and GRAND-SERAUCOURT was blown up under orders of 109 Bde. Map Refce Sheet 66C NW G 1 b 9.2	
		3.15 AM.	Bridge C over river on Cinder Track running from West End of SERAUCOURT to Canal between HAMEL and HAMEL LOCK blown up Map Refce of bridge Sheet 66C NW G 7 b 8.8.	
		3.45 AM.	Bridge 33C and foot bridge at HAMEL LOCK blown up under orders from 109th Infy Bde	
			All above bridges were very successfully demolished, the gaps being much bigger than was anticipated and the piers of the Trestles so damaged as to be of no further use for rebuilding.	
		7.0 AM	2/Lt NORMAN R.E. reported completion of demolition of all bridges in HAMEL-SERAUCOURT group. He brought his section back without casualties and brought back the four exploders.	
			In connection with above demolition 2/Lt NORMAN, 2/Corpl RAINBIRD and 2/Cpl ROBSON did exceptionally good work.	AL
		12.0 Noon	Company with Transport moved through HAM to GOLANCOURT	
			Lt R.E. WALSH R.E. and No 3 Section took over the demolition of Bridges between HAM and OLLEZY from CORPS R.E.	
			All bridges were successfully blown up with the exception of a railway bridge which had not been prepared by Corps R.E. for demolition.	
	23.3.18		The first bridge was blown about 12.30 AM under orders from Infantry holding the HAM-OLLEZY line of Trenches.	
			The last bridge viz the heavy bridge on the HAM-NOYON road was blown up about 7.30 AM	
			In connection with these demolitions Lt R.E. WALSH R.E. Sgt GRICE and 2nd Corpl HAMILTON did very good work.	
			Mounted Section under Lt WALSH RE moved to a field near FRETOY	
			The four dismounted Sections under Capt H. GOOCH. R.E moved to P 29 b Central and under instructions from Major LOWE of M.G.Bn dug a number of fire bays in echelon and manned them. Line extended in front of BORNEUIL CHATEAU from 29 a Central to 29 b Central approximately	
			about midnight as Enemy had broken through on right the three Field Coys withdrew under instructions of Major LOWE and took up a position in P 29 a Central. 122 Field & 150 Field Coys being on the right in P 29 b and d. M.G. Company who were previously on the right of 122 Field Coy and the Composite Bn on left of this unit withdrew thus leaving both flanks of the Field Coys undefended	AL

A5834 Wt. W4973/M687 750,000 8/16 D. D. & L. Ltd. Forms/C.2118/13.

Army Form C. 2118.

WAR DIARY
or
INTELLIGENCE SUMMARY.
(*Erase heading not required.*)

121st Field Coy R.E.

Instructions regarding War Diaries and Intelligence Summaries are contained in F. S. Regs., Part II. and the Staff Manual respectively. Title pages will be prepared in manuscript.

Place	Date	Hour	Summary of Events and Information	Remarks and references to Appendices
	24.3.18		Shortly after dawn LT W.H. BLAGDENRE was wounded by rifle bullet in the arm.	
			French patrols arrived & reported their position behind.	
			Three Field Coys withdrew to French outposts about 800x in rear and immediately deployed and took up a position between the woods North of FLAVY at P34b central to P35b5.0. as many men were seen coming over the crest west of the CHATEAU. Whilst the men were digging themselves Capt Gooch collected several stragglers both officers and O.R. including two Lewis guns and one Vickers Gun and posted them all in various defensive positions.	
			Major C.A. EMERY of 89th Infy Bde who appeared on the scene took charge of a large number of stragglers and at the request of Capt GOOCH took them over to the west side of the wood as it was reported that Enemy Cavalry were coming that way. He established a line there. Enemy aeroplanes flying very low reconnoitred the position, and apparently took the information back as the next Enemy attack was on the right and left of the positions taken up by the Field Coys & stragglers.	
			About 8.0PM Major R.A.H. LEWIN arrived back from leave and took over command of the dismounted men.	
			Capt GOOCH returned to FRETOY to take charge of mounted section and Transport.	
			LT WALSH who had been with the horse lines under Major J.H. OTWAY RE prepared a bridge for demolition 600x west of FRETOY and handed it over to a T.M. detachment posted there by division to guard the bridge.	
			LT WALSH ~~rode~~ arrived with Major LEWIN to take charge of his section	H.L.
	25.3.18	1.0AM	Horse lines moved to MARGNY-AUX-CERISE arriving at 5.0AM	
		2.0AM.	In front of FLAVY the French dispositions being completed the Field Coys were moved to the 4th line	
		3.0AM.	Orders were received for unit to withdraw and march to BEAULIEU near FRENICHES. Unit arrived at 6.0AM	
		11.30AM	Men marched to HAVRICOURT and later in the day was joined by Transport.	
		7.0PM	Unit under 107th Infy Bde marched GUERBIGNY arriving at 3.0AM.	H.L.
	26.3.18	10.0AM	Mounted Section under Capt GOOCH moved to GRISVESNES. Tool carts and water cart left with dismounted men.	
		12 noon	Dismounted men under 107th Bde took up position in Q23c ~~at~~ in old trenches near ANDECHY - GUERBIGNY road	H.L.

A5834 Wt. W4973/M687 750,000 8/16 D. D. & L. Ltd. Forms/C.2118/13.

Instructions regarding War Diaries and Intelligence Summaries are contained in F. S. Regs., Part II. and the Staff Manual respectively. Title pages will be prepared in manuscript.

WAR DIARY
or
~~INTELLIGENCE SUMMARY.~~
(Erase heading not required.)

121st Field Coy R.E.

Army Form C. 2118.

Place	Date	Hour	Summary of Events and Information	Remarks and references to Appendices
	26.3.18		Water cart and tool carts were taken by 2/Lt POTTS to BECQUIGNY and brigaded under Lt TATE.	
			2/Lt POTTS reported to 107th Bde HQ and with Brigade Major inspected the line of trenches and gun pits south of & west of ERCHES Q4b 1.3 to K35 6.7.	
			107th Bde moved onto the selected line on west side of village at dusk. This unit was between the 15th RIR and the 16th R.I.R. (21st Entrenching Bn)	
			There was some M.G fire and T.M fire on these positions during the night.	
			LT. WALSH R.E. went out in charge of a patrol and discovered that Enemy transport was travelling up and down the AMIENS-ROYE road north of ERCHES. This traffic continued all night. The information was given to Bde H.Q.	HG
	27.3.18		An hour after dawn two British aeroplanes flew over the trenches and made signals that were not understood. They then flew over ERCHES firing M.Guns into Enemy line & were fired on by heavy M.G fire from ERCHES thus giving indication that the Enemy was in strength in the village.	
		9.0 AM	107 Bde trenches were bombarded by 4.2 TM and rifle grenades. There were several casualties. Enemy attacked on right was engaged with rifle & L.G. fire.	HG
		12 NOON	Major McCALLUM of 21st Entrenching Bn passed down a message to say that the troops on his right had withdrawn.	
			121 Field Coy then withdrew from the right & were caught in a heavy barrage of shell & MG fire. The Bn became divided right and left of ARVILLERS. Major LEWIN & 2/Lt NORMAN were both severely wounded but were carried to A.D.S.	
			There was no artillery assistance in this sector at any time.	
			LT WALSH was also wounded and did not get away.	
			C.S.M GAMBLE and SGT McINNES did good work collecting the stragglers and eventually collected 42 men and posted them on the left of the village on left of 1st R.I.R. A Brigadier General of 30th division ordered these troops to take up position in R25 & 26. There were details of 15th & 16th R.I.R. with this party.	
			Part of transport was sent to [illegible]	
	28.3.18	4.10 PM	Order was received to withdraw 36th Division from line & 107th Bde [illegible] BOURDON	
			Total casualties in these operations were 3 officers wounded, 1 officer wounded & missing, 11 OR missing, 26 wounded, 6 wounded & missing, 2 wounded & remained at duty.	HG

A5834 Wt. W4973/M687 750,000 8/16 D. D. & L. Ltd. Forms/C.2118/13.

Instructions regarding War Diaries and Intelligence Summaries are contained in F. S. Regs., Part II. and the Staff Manual respectively. Title pages will be prepared in manuscript.

WAR DIARY

or

~~INTELLIGENCE SUMMARY.~~

(Erase heading not required.)

121st Field Coy R.E.

Army Form C. 2118.

Place	Date	Hour	Summary of Events and Information	Remarks and references to Appendices
	28.3.18		During these operations excellent patrol work was done by Cpl King, L/Cpl Gowdy, and L/Cpl Drennan. Nos 3 and 4 sections under 2/Lt POTTS had joined Major ALLEN of 16th R.I.R. and withdrawn to HANGEST-EN-SANTERRE and remained there until orders were received to withdraw to HARGICOURT and eventually to SOURDON	JH
		3.0 PM	Coy moved to EPAGNY	
		6.30 PM	Transport lines moved to wood N W of CHAUSSY-EPAGNY	
	29.3.18		Coy moved to VARENNES	JH
	30.3.18		Transport moved to ALLERY, staying overnight moved to DARGNIES on 31.3.18.	JH
			Dismounted men marched to SALEUX and entrained, detrained at LONGROY-GAMACHES and marched	JH
	31.3.18		to DARGNIES. Transport arrived at 7.0 PM.	

[illegible] Capt R.E.

for O.C. 121 Field Coy R.E.

A5834 Wt. W4973/M687 750,000 8/16 D. D. & L. Ltd. Forms/C.2118/13.

36th Divisional Engineers

121st FIELD COMPANY R.E. ::: APRIL 1918.

Confidential

Vol 31

War Diary
of
121 Field Coy - R E
for month of April 1918

Army Form C. 2118.

Instructions regarding War Diaries and Intelligence Summaries are contained in F. S. Regs., Part II. and the Staff Manual respectively. Title pages will be prepared in manuscript.

WAR DIARY
or
INTELLIGENCE SUMMARY.

(Erase heading not required.)

Place	Date	Hour	Summary of Events and Information	Remarks and references to Appendices

A5834 Wt. W4973/M687 750,000 8/16 D. D. & L. Ltd. Forms/C.2118/13.

Instructions regarding War Diaries and Intelligence Summaries are contained in F. S. Regs., Part II. and the Staff Manual respectively. Title pages will be prepared in manuscript.

WAR DIARY 121st Field Coy R.E.

~~or INTELLIGENCE SUMMARY.~~

(Erase heading not required.)

Army Form C. 2118.

Place	Date	Hour	Summary of Events and Information	Remarks and references to Appendices
	1/4/18		Whole Company at DARGNIES Strength 156 including 14 men on leave and 2 on detachment and transport & personnel sent to [illegible]. Employed in checking mobilisation stores and equipment	
	2/4/18		4 men rejoined after previously being reported as missing. Transport & personnel sent to [illegible] rejoined.	
	3/4/18		Transport moved off at 10.45 PM and dismounted men at 12.30 AM to FEUQUIERES to entrain	
	4/4/18		Arrived at PROVEN at 11.30 PM and detrained	
	5/4/18		Men taken in lorries & Transport followed to HOSPITAL FARM Camp near ELVERDINGHE	
	6/4/18		2 men sent to REIGERSBURG to work delousing plant. 1 off and 1 NCO went forward to take over work from 409th Field Coy RE	
	7/4/18		Coy moved Horse lines to MORAT CAMP Sheet 28 B30 b0.3. Dismounted men to CANAL BANK Sheet 28 C25 Central. 1 M.A.H. 1 Reinforcement joined	
	8/4/18		Coy employed in Billet improvements and making gas proof doors	
	9/4/18		Work taken over consisted of preparing formation and laying DECAUVILLE Track from MINTY FARM in Sheet 28 C10 to RETOUR CROSS ROADS in Sheet 28 V19 near POELCAPELLE. C.S.M admitted to hospital. News received that 2/LT TY NORMAN R.E. died of wounds. 10 men of 15th R.I.R attached as working party.	
	10/4/18		49 Reinforcements joined the Coy. 4 men admitted to hospital. Work as above	
	11/4/18		Strength of unit now 206. Work as above	

A5834 Wt. W4973/M687 750,000 8/16 D. D. & L. Ltd. Forms/C.2118/13.

Instructions regarding War Diaries and Intelligence Summaries are contained in F. S. Regs., Part II. and the Staff Manual respectively. Title pages will be prepared in manuscript.

WAR DIARY 121st Field Coy R.E.

or

~~INTELLIGENCE~~ SUMMARY.

(Erase heading not required.)

Army Form C. 2118.

Place	Date	Hour	Summary of Events and Information	Remarks and references to Appendices
	12/4/18		H.Q. and 4 Sections moved to KEMPTON PARK SOUTH. Horse Lines remained at MURAT CAMP	JHG.
			1 Man wounded by HE & admitted to hospital.	
	13/4/18		Sections employed on billet improvements. CSM [illegible] evacuated. Two sections employed on making entanglements in the evening	JHG.
	14/4/18		Half No 4 Sect employed in making a dam across the STEENBEEK. Rest of Coy employed in making portable wire entanglements to fill gaps in belts of wire where roads cross belts. Half No 2 Section employed on divisional O.P. at light at C15a6.4.	JHG.
	15/4/18		Horse lines under Capt H. GOOCH R.E. moved to CARDOEN Camp at A18b2.0. Forward horse lines at MURAT Camp with 2 Tool Carts 1 Pontoon Wagon & 3 Limbers & 24 animals.	JHG.
			Dismounted sections employed with infantry in construction of a new front line running from CANOE Trench at C16b7.8 in front of ~~[illegible]~~ OBLONG farm C16b5.0 through C16a3.8 & C16a4.5, C16a7.2 thence to CALAHAN reserve Trench at C22b6.5.	
			The line consisted of four strong points each holding 2 sections. All work was breast work with A frames. The line was also wired with 2 double apron fences. After completion of work the Coy took up new billets in Canal Bank at C25a8.3.	
			3 men who were wounded on 27/3/18 rejoined unit	
	16/4/18		At dawn the Division withdrew to line WEST of the STEENBEEK	JHG.
			Location of different detachments of Coy as on 15th.	
			Sections 3 & 4 employed as on 15th & in making a [illegible] block in CANOE Trench at C16b7.8	
	17/4/18		Section 1 & 2 went out to proceed with strengthening of new line but just after commencement of work received information from Brigade that enemy had occupied forward slope immediately west of STEENBEEK and consequently no further work could be done in daylight on new front line. Sections withdrawn to Camp.	JHG.

A5834 Wt. W4973/M687 750,000 8/16 D. D. & L. Ltd. Forms/C.2118/13.

Instructions regarding War Diaries and Intelligence Summaries are contained in F. S. Regs., Part II. and the Staff Manual respectively. Title pages will be prepared in manuscript.

WAR DIARY 121st Field Coy R.E.
or
~~INTELLIGENCE SUMMARY.~~
(*Erase heading not required.*)

Army Form C. 2118.

Place	Date	Hour	Summary of Events and Information	Remarks and references to Appendices
	18/4/18		No day work. 1 Section employed with 50 Infy in levelling down & filling in CANDY Trench from C16 b 80.75 to C17 a 1.6. 1 & 4 Section moved from CANAL BANK to CARDOEN CAMP. 1 M.A.H.	H.G.
	19/4/18		Nos 2 + 3 Sections employed in putting E bank of Canal from C19 a 2.5 to I 1 b 77 in a state of defence. This work consisted of 8 platoon posts guarding bridge heads & complete wiring over whole front & along water's edge.	H.G.
	20/4/18		Nos 2 + 3 Sections employed as on 19th. 1 Reinforcement arrived. 1 M.D.H. 1 & 4 Sections [illegible]	H.G.
	21/4/18		1 & 4 Section + HQ with horse lines moved from CARDOEN CAMP and Nos 2 + 3 Sections from CANAL BANK all to BROMWELL CAMP B13 a 5.3. Work on CANAL BANK handed over to 150 Field Coy RE.	H.G.
	22/4/18		Whole Coy bathed at REIGERSBERG. The O.C + officers reconnoitred with CRE + GSO1 new defence line. 1 M.A.H.	H.G.
	23/4/18		4 Sections with working party of 200 Infy engaged on organisation preparation and wiring of BRIELEN defence line B23 a in front of BRIELEN to B28 c. 1 M.D.H.	H.G.
	24/4/18		Work as on 23rd. Working Party 400. 2 men struck off strength	H.G.
	25/4/18		do do Material transported by lorry, horse transport and light railway close to site of work.	H.G.
	26/4/18		do No working party	H.G.
	27/4/18		do Working party 2 Coys Infy up till midday	H.G.
	28/4/18		Main horse lines at CAMBS[illegible] moved back to X Camp A16 c 2.5. Dismounted men & limbers, water cart & 16 animals remain at BROMWELL	H.G.
	29/4/18		3 Sections employed on constructing bridge over POPERINGHE CANAL at A21 a 5.0 to carry Field Guns. Bridge completed in 1 day. 1 Reinforcement	H.G.
	30/4/18		4 Sections and 2 Companies of Pioneers employed on BRIELEN DEFENCES. Work consisted of improvement of wire, [illegible] & dugouts and connecting up the various posts so as to make a continuous line. Work as on 29th. Working party of 1 Coy of Pioneers only. 2/Lt WEIGHTON admitted to hospital. 1 Man struck off strength	H.G.

H Goech Capt RE
for OC 121 Field Coy R.E.

A5834 Wt. W4973/M687 750,000 8/16 D. D. & L. Ltd. Forms/C.2118/13.

Confidential

Vol 32

War Diary

of

121 Field Company R.E.

from 1-5-18 to 31-5-18

Instructions regarding War Diaries and Intelligence Summaries are contained in F. S. Regs., Part II. and the Staff Manual respectively. Title pages will be prepared in manuscript.

WAR DIARY
or
~~INTELLIGENCE SUMMARY.~~
(Erase heading not required.)

121st Field Coy R.E.

Army Form C. 2118.

Place	Date	Hour	Summary of Events and Information	Remarks and references to Appendices
	1/5/18		HQ, 4 dismounted sections and part of Transport at BRONWELL CAMP B13 a 5.3. Sheet 28. CQM Stores & rear horse-lines at X Camp A16 C 2.5. Major Otway and Lt Wrighton still in hospital. 4 Sections with 1 Company pioneers employed on improvement of BRIELEN DEFENCES. Work consisted of making a continuous line between 41st Division Sheet 28 I 5 b & BELGIANS in B 23 a. Almost impossible to dig [illegible] more than 1 ft anywhere so line has to be breastwork. Improvement of existing posts, dugouts and wire put in hand. 1 M.D.H.	H.G.
	2/5/18		Work as above. Clearing of drains round positions commenced. Working party 2 Coys of Infy in addition to 1 Coy pioneers. 2 Men admitted to Hospital.	H.G.
	3/5/18		Work as above. 1 M.A.H.	H.G.
	4/5/18		" " " 1 M.D.H. Cpl Robson, L Cpl Hamilton and L Cpl Rainton awarded Military Medal.	H.G.
	5/5/18		" " " 2 M.D.H.	H.G.
	6/5/18		" " "	H.G.
	7/5/18		Very heavy rain prevented work in morning. 4 Sections turned out at 1.30. Work on drainage & improvement of breastworks as above. 1 M.D.H.	H.G.
	8/5/18		Work as above. Interfered with to some extent by shelling. No working party as pioneers were being bathed. 1 M.D.H.	H.G.
	9/5/18		Work as above. 1 Coy of pioneers as working party. 4 M.A.H.	H.G.
	10/5/18		1 Section commenced work on FANTASIA FARM cutting large elephants to accommodate Bde HQ, Sheet 28 B 21 d 5.5. 3 Sections with 1 Coy pioneers still employed on BRIELEN DEFENCES. 6 Reinforcements joined unit.	H.G.
	11/5/18		Work as above. Working party 1 Coy of pioneers only owing to Infy relief. 1 M.D.H. 3 M.A.H.	H.G.
	12/5/18		" " " " 1 Coy of pioneers & 1 Coy Infy.	H.G.
	13/5/18		"	H.G.
	14/5/18		" " 2 M.A.H.	H.G.
	15/5/18		" 2 M.A.H.	

A5834 Wt. W4973/M687 750,000 8/16 D. D. & L. Ltd. Forms/C.2118/13.

Instructions regarding War Diaries and Intelligence Summaries are contained in F. S. Regs., Part II. and the Staff Manual respectively. Title Pages will be prepared in manuscript.

WAR DIARY

~~or~~

~~INTELLIGENCE SUMMARY~~

(Erase heading not required.)

121st Field Coy R.E.

Army Form C. 2118.

Place	Date	Hour	Summary of Events and Information	Remarks and references to Appendices
	16/5/18		Four Sections still on BRIELEN DEFENCES. Capt Gooch and 2 Section Officers went over GREEN LINE defences with O.C 122 Field Coy & take over this work. 1 M.A.H.	JHG.
	17/5/18.		No 4 Section moved to billets in CANAL BANK & became attached to R.F.A for work on Emplacements & O Ps. No 3 Section took charge of all work on BRIELEN line. Working party 2 Coys of pioneers & 2 Coys of Infy. No 1 & 2 Sections working on GREEN line. No 2 Section took charge of all work on Trenches in Sheet 28 B 20 and 26. No 1 Section took over construction of Bn HQ at B20 c 2.5. Bn HQ at B26 a 2.5 RAP. at B25c b 1.4. Bde HQ at A24 a 4.2 Bridge over KEMMELBEEK at B20 b 2.3. Repairs of dam at B14 b 4.4. Bde HQ at B21 d Centre. CAPT. H. GOOCH promoted to Tempy. Major. All these HQ. consist of Big Elephants inside farm houses covered with earth & bursters. 2 M.D.H. CSM BROWN joined unit. Two large bombs dropped on Camp at night & wounded 2 men, 2 mules & destroyed mess cart & 1 limber. 2 M.D.H.	JHG.
	18/5/18.		Work as above. Working parties 2 Coys of pioneers on BRIELEN defences. { No working party on GREEN LINE except 1 platoon wiring 80 RAMC working on the various H.Q. Major OTWAY returned from hospital. 2 drivers wounded by Enemy bomb at night. 2 mules wounded also.	JHG
	19/5/18		REST. DAY. Weather extremely hot. 1 M.DH. 1 Man struck off strength	JHG
	20/5/18		Work as above. Strength of working parties on GREEN LINE 750 Infy & Pioneers on BRIELEN LINE 350 " " on Dugout construction 80 RAMC.	JHG
	21/5/18		Work as above. Work on GREEN LINE all concentrated on front line. No work being done on support line. 1 MAH.	JHG
	22/5/18		" " " II LT POTTS promoted on Special List. Major J.H. OTWAY and 2 and [illegible] Sgt MOORE R. mentioned in despatches.	JHG
	23/5/18		" " II LT DAVIES relieved Lt Potts at CANAL Bank. 6 Men Evacuated. 1 M.A.H.	JHG
	24/5/18		" " " Heavy rain interfered with work. Bridge over KEMMEL BEEK at B20 b 2.3 completed.	JHG
	25/5/18		" " " 1 M.A.H. 2nd Cpl Howorth rejoined.	JHG
	26/5/18		REST. DAY. 1 Driver reinforcement from hospital.	JHG
	27/5/18		Work as on 25th. II Lt Weighton evacuated. 1 M.A.H. 2 Drivers joined unit	JHG.

2449 Wt. W14957/M90 750,000 1/16 J.B.C. & A. Forms/C.2118/12.

Instructions regarding War Diaries and Intelligence Summaries are contained in F. S. Regs., Part II. and the Staff Manual respectively. Title Pages will be prepared in manuscript.

WAR DIARY
or
~~INTELLIGENCE~~ SUMMARY
(Erase heading not required.)

121st Field Coy R.E.

Army Form C. 2118.

Place	Date	Hour	Summary of Events and Information	Remarks and references to Appendices
	28/5/18		Work as on 27th	
	29/5/18.		Coy Moved dismounted portion. O.C + 3 Sections to CANAL BANK C19C3.3. Major GOOCH + 1 dismounted Section moved to horse lines at X Camp A16C2.5. Work forward taken over from 122nd Field Coy. Consisting of preparation of WIELTJE ~~&~~ mined dugouts (C28c) for demolition and also dugouts at HILL TOP Sheet 28 C21d. Screening of PERTH ROAD in B30 b and B29d	
	30/5/18		Preparation of CANAL Bridges for demolition, assisting 107 Infy Bde in preparation of forward posts. Laying of charges to form road craters at cross roads C22C - C21C - C27a - C20C - C20 C13 - C25 a3-8. Dismounted Section at horse lines engaged in cleaning up transport, erection of cookhouse & general Camp improvements. Forward work as above. Four reinforcements joined from base. 1 M.A.H.	
	31/5/18.		Work as above. Weather very hot. No 4 Section at horse lines engaged in Training. 1 M.A.H.	

31/5/18.

H Gooch Major R.E.
for O.C. 121 Field Coy R.E.

2449 Wt. W14957/M90 750,000 1/16 J.B.C. & A. Forms/C.2118/12.

Confidential Vol 33

War Diary

of

121st Field Company RE

1-6-18 to 30-6-18

Instructions regarding War Diaries and Intelligence Summaries are contained in F. S. Regs., Part II. and the Staff Manual respectively. Title pages will be prepared in manuscript.

WAR DIARY
or
~~INTELLIGENCE~~ SUMMARY.
(Erase heading not required.)

121st Field Coy R.E.

Army Form C. 2118.

Place	Date	Hour	Summary of Events and Information	Remarks and references to Appendices
	1/6/18		O.C with Nos 1.2. & 3 Sections at CANAL BANK Sheet 28 Dugout No 217	
			Major Gooch with mounted Section HQ and No 4 Section at X Camp Sheet 28	
			No 1 Section employed on Brigade Work in front line and on Switch Line joining CANAL BANK DEFENCES with line of Belgian Division on left.	
			No 2 Section being responsible for maintenance and upkeep of Bridges No 3A, 3B, Rly 4, 4A, 5 & 6 over Canal. Also responsible for maintaining demolition charges on those bridges in condition and for demolishing the bridges if necessary. For this purpose patrols are maintained on the Bridges night & day. The approaches to Bridge 5 are being cleared to allow Field Artillery to pass	
			No 3 Section took over charge of Demolition charges in WEILTJE mined dugouts C28b - HILLTOP Dugout C21a - MAROCCO Pill box C19c also demolition charges to form road craters at cross roads C22c - C21c - C27a - C20c - C25a 3.8 and others west of CANAL	
			For this purpose 4 men live in HILLTOP and 1 NCO and 4 men live in WEILTJE	
			Remainder of section employed in screening road from C25a 3.8 to B29 & a 7.5.	
			No 4 Section employed on Training	H.G.
			Strength of Company 209. 1 Man Evacuated.	
	2/6/18		Clearing of approaches to Bridge 5 Completed.	
			Some men employed on repairs to Bridge 4 which had been damaged by a direct hit	
			Conference of Os C Field Coys & OC pioneers at CRE's HQ reference handing over of work to Belgians.	H.G.

A5834 Wt. W4973/M687 750,000 8/16 D. D. & L. Ltd. Forms/C.2118/13.

Instructions regarding War Diaries and Intelligence Summaries are contained in F. S. Regs., Part II. and the Staff Manual respectively. Title pages will be prepared in manuscript.

WAR DIARY
or
~~INTELLIGENCE~~ SUMMARY.
(*Erase heading not required.*)

121st Field Coy R.E.

Army Form C. 2118.

Place	Date	Hour	Summary of Events and Information	Remarks and references to Appendices
	3/6/18		Work as above. Work on HILLTOP and WEILTJE and Bridge demolitions continued but no other work. Remainder of men employed in cleaning their equipment. 1 officer + 1 platoon of the Engineers of the 12th Belgian Division arrived at CANAL BANK at 7.0 PM and occupied billets on CANAL Bank West. HILLTOP, WEILTJE and Road Craters E of CANAL as shown above handed over at night to BELGIAN ENGINEERS. 1 Man Evacuated	J.H.G.
	4/6/18		Whole company moved to BALL Camp SHEET 27 L3 b 3.7 after handing over remainder of work as shown above to BELGIAN Engineers. Nos 1, 2 + 3 Sections moved by train from BRIELEN to POPERINGHE + marched to BALL CAMP. No 4 Section + HQ marched from X Camp to BALL CAMP. 7 Reinforcements joined Coy. 1 MAH.	J.H.G.
	5/6/18		Dismounted men employed in Kit Inspection + smartening up. 1 Reinforcement from Hospital	J.H.G.
	6/6/18		Dismounted men engaged in Physical Exercise + drill + general training to smarten them up.	J.H.G.
	7/6/18		do do.	J.H.G.
	8/6/18		do do	J.H.G.
	9/6/18		Full church parade of 3 Field Coys followed by ~~an~~ inspection by the CRE. 2 Reinforcements from Hospital	J.H.G.
	10/6/18		Dismounted men employed Training. C.S.M. PATE. J joined as reinforcement. 1 MAH.	J.H.G.
	11/6/18		do 3 MAH	J.H.G.
				J.H.G.

A5834 Wt. W4973/M687 750,000 8/16 D. D. & L. Ltd. Forms/C.2118/13.

Instructions regarding War Diaries and Intelligence Summaries are contained in F. S. Regs., Part II. and the Staff Manual respectively. Title pages will be prepared in manuscript.

WAR DIARY
or
~~INTELLIGENCE SUMMARY.~~
(Erase heading not required.)

Army Form C. 2118.

Place	Date	Hour	Summary of Events and Information	Remarks and references to Appendices
	12/6/18		Whole company moved to PRICE CAMP Sheet 27 F 7 b 5. Men accommodated in Nissen huts & tents. Horses on open picket line in field. 3 M.A.H.	H.G.
	13/6/18		Company employed on camp improvement erection of cook house and harness sheds. 15 men excused duty with influenza. OC + two officers + section sergeants reconnoitred GREEN LINE near VLAMERTINGHE on which 150th Field Coy was working	H.G.
	14/6/18		Work on Green Line taken over from 150th Field Coy. Men proceeded by train from PUGWASH FARM E 6 b central to MISSION STATION ~~B27~~ Sheet 28 B 27 d then marched to work. Men had to leave camp at 3:30 AM + got back at 3:35 PM. Work consisted of revetting, building up parapets and paradors and duckboarding of front line and support line between railway at H 8 b and H 14 a 2.8 Sheet 28. When taken over the work on an average was about 70% complete. 1 Company 16th R.I.R (Pioneers) and 2 Companies Infantry placed at disposal of O.C. Field Coy for this work all this work was under direction of CRE Corps Troops.	H.G.
	~~15/6/18~~ 15/6/18		30 men excused duty with influenza which is very prevalent in the district. Work as above. 2 M.D.H. 1 Man went on leave.	H.G.
	16/6/18		Sunday. No work. Church parade in morning.	H.G.
	17/6/18		No further work done on VLAMERTINGHE LINE. The company with 1 Company of Pioneers and 2 Companies of Infantry was employed on EAST POPERINGHE line from H 22 Central Sheet 28 to POPERINGHE – VLAMERTINGHE road. Work consisted of clearance of all crops, hedges, [illegible] and other obstacles for 300x in front of front line. 1 M.D.H.	H.G.

A5834 Wt. W4973/M687 750,000 8/16 D. D. & L. Ltd. Forms/C.2118/13.

Instructions regarding War Diaries and Intelligence Summaries are contained in F. S. Regs., Part II. and the Staff Manual respectively. Title pages will be prepared in manuscript.

WAR DIARY
or
~~INTELLIGENCE SUMMARY.~~

(Erase heading not required.)

121st Field Coy R.E.

Army Form C. 2118.

Place	Date	Hour	Summary of Events and Information	Remarks and references to Appendices
	18/6/18		Work as on 14th. Numbers of men employed the same. No. of influenza cases decreasing.	H.G.
	19/6/18		Work as above. A low belt of wire comprised of 2 plain fences with cross fences commenced. This is additional to the two double apron fences already existing.	
			1 M.D.H. 3 Hospital Reinforcements.	H.G.
	20/6/18		Work as above. No. of sick in unit now reduced to 7.	H.G.
			C.Q.M.S. LARMOUR. E.M. awarded the M.S.M.	H.G.
	21/6/18		Work and number of men employed as above. 3 men evacuated	H.G.
	22/6/18		1 M.A.H.	H.G.
	23/6/18		Sunday. Church parades at 11.0 AM. No men on works.	
	24/6/18		Work and number of men employed as on 22nd. 1 Sapper sent on course of Cooking for officers mess	H.G.
	25/5/18		1 R.A.H.	
	~~26~~		Major J. H. OTWAY. R.E. Transferred to 150 Field Coy R.E. to take command of that unit	
			Major H. GOOCH M.C. R.E. appointed O.C. 121 Field Coy vice Major OTWAY	H.G.
			LIEUT T. K. KNOX M.C. Transferred from 122 Field Coy to 121 Field Coy to act as second-in-command of that unit.	
	26/6/18		Work as above. Working parties same but no. of sappers reduced by 30 to receive 1 days instruction in musketry under a Sgt Musketry Instructor.	
	27/6/18		No. 2 Section took over the construction of Bde H.Q. at KNOLLYS FARM Sheet 28 H.7.C.7.0. Structure consists to consist of 10 chambers built inside a barn. Interior consisting of framework of pit props and rails sheeted with trough plates and built up with bags of rubble & earth. Roof to be made in one span	
			No. 4 Section employed on strengthening a shelter for Bn H.Q. at A.21.a.3.6 to make it 5.9 proof.	

Instructions regarding War Diaries and Intelligence Summaries are contained in F. S. Regs., Part II. and the Staff Manual respectively. Title pages will be prepared in manuscript.

WAR DIARY
or
~~INTELLIGENCE~~ SUMMARY. 121st Field Coy R E

(*Erase heading not required.*)

Army Form C. 2118.

Place	Date	Hour	Summary of Events and Information	Remarks and references to Appendices
	27/6/18	Contd	Nos 1 & 3 Sections, less 30 men undergoing musketry instruction, employed East POPERINGHE line as described above on 17th. Working party for this work same as on 17th.	HG
	28/6/18		Work as on 27th. Working party same.	HG
	29/6/18		Work as on 28th. 1 M.D.H.	HG
	30/6/18		Work as on 29th. 2 NCOs went to Army Rest Camp for 14 days	HG

30/6/18

H Gooch Major RE
O.C. 121 Field Coy R.E.

A5834 Wt. W4973/M687 750,000 8/16 D. D. & L. Ltd. Forms/C.2118/13.

Confidential Vol 34

War Diary

of

121st Field Company RE

from 1-V-18 to 31-V-18

Instructions regarding War Diaries and Intelligence Summaries are contained in F. S. Regs., Part II. and the Staff Manual respectively. Title pages will be prepared in manuscript.

WAR DIARY
or
INTELLIGENCE SUMMARY.
(*Erase heading not required.*)

Army Form C. 2118.

121 Field Company R.E.

Place	Date	Hour	Summary of Events and Information	Remarks and references to Appendices
	1/7/18		No work done by company; Divisional horse show held at PROVEN aerodrome	TKK
	2/7/18		Company moved to BALL CAMP - Sheet 27 L3 b 3.7, No 1 & 2 sections employed on construction of Bde HQ at KNOLLYS FARM Sheet 28. H7 c 7.0. No 3 Section employed on E. POPERINGHE LINE from H22 Central sheet 28 to POPERINGHE - VLAMERTINGHE ROAD. No 4 Section employed strengthening shelter for Bn HQ at A24 a 0.6, working parties on E. POPERINGHE LINE consist of 2 coys Infantry (188 Bde) and 1 Coy Pioneers (4 R.R.) Sappers returned to BALL CAMP by walk on completion of work. No 10112 Sgt Smith posted to Company.	TKK
	3/7/18		Company with transport moved by road to O30 c 0.4 sheet 27 about two miles south of CASSEL	TKK
	4/7/18		Inspection of gas helmets, identity discs, field dressings etc. and gas helmet drill.	TKK
	5/7/18		Gas drill and general training	TKK
	6/7/18		Company on general training, officers went forward to take over work from the 7/2 Company French Engineers. 2/Lt Davies & Cpl Crawford proceeded to Rouen on course of Instruction in Field Engineering	TKK
	7/7/18.		General Training in morning, the whole company with transport moved to the new HQ at Q 32 b 70.70 Sheet 27 in the afternoon, OC with four sections moved up at night and took over billets and work from 7/2 French Engineers, OC & sec 3 & 4 being billeted in dug outs at R26 c 20-20. No 1 sec in dugouts at R33 b 5.0. No 2 Sec in houses at R27 a 70-95.	TKK

A5834 Wt. W4973/M687 750,000 8/16 D. D. & L. Ltd. Forms/C.2118/13.

Army Form C. 2118.

Instructions regarding War Diaries and Intelligence Summaries are contained in F. S. Regs., Part II. and the Staff Manual respectively. Title pages will be prepared in manuscript.

WAR DIARY
or
INTELLIGENCE SUMMARY.
(*Erase heading not required.*)

Place	Date	Hour	Summary of Events and Information	Remarks and references to Appendices
	8/7/18		The company is employed on following work Mined dug out for ADS at R20 d 5.7 constructing additional chamber to Bde HQ dugout at R27 a 1.9., completion of mined dugout for Bde HQ at R33 d 4.9., tunnelled dug out at R26 c 10.20 ditto at R33 d 5.9., working on line running through R33 b & c other work consists of improvement of men billets Working parties 50 pioneers on wiring 50 pioneers on mined dug outs & 15 infantry on mined dug outs	TKK
	9/7/18		Work as above and improvement of Coy HQ at R34 c 5.4 commenced	TKK
	10/7/18		Work as above, Bunking of Cellar for Coy HQ at X 4 a 4 3 started 1 NCO & 2 men attached to Bde holding line to assist in dug out construction. Shortage of materials and bad weather interferes with progress of work.	TKK
	11/7/18		Work same as on 10/7/18, bunking of cellar completed	TKK
	12/7/18		Work as above, gas proof doors put on entrance to Bde HQ at R33 d 5.9	TKK
	13/7/18		Work as above Improvement to Coy HQ at R34 c 5.4 completed	TKK

A5834 Wt. W4973/M687 750,000 8/16 D. D. & L. Ltd. Forms/C.2118/13.

Instructions regarding War Diaries and Intelligence Summaries are contained in F. S. Regs., Part II. and the Staff Manual respectively. Title Pages will be prepared in manuscript.

WAR DIARY
or
INTELLIGENCE SUMMARY

(Erase heading not required.)

Army Form C. 2118.

Place	Date	Hour	Summary of Events and Information	Remarks and references to Appendices
	14/7/18		Work as before, working parties the same	TKK
	15/7/18		do Two OR to rest camp Audisselles	TKK
	16/7/18		Work as before, strengthening of Bde HQ at X 5 a.5.8. started	TKK
	17/7/18		Improvement and strengthening of Battery Commanders posts at R 26 d 77 and R 27. b. 20.05 commenced, Labour and materials supplied by RFA. Reconnaissance of BLUE LINE between X 4. c. 8.3 and R. 35. c. 98. made & line marked out with tracing tapes, other work as before. Two men admitted to hospital.	TKK
	18/7/18.		Work on blue line commenced at night by 4 Coys, about 300 men, of 15th RIR work consists of digging trench 3'-6" deep, clearing crops in front and wiring Hostile guns fairly active, other work as above.	TKK
	19/7/18		G.O.C division & CRE inspected BLUE LINE at night, a good deal of enemy gas shelling at night, working parties as above.	TKK
	20/7/18		Work as above, OC & GSO1 reconnoitred right end of proposed line connecting BLUE LINE to 9th Div Support line. One OR proceeded on leave	TKK
	21/7/18		Work commenced on Coy HQ at R 35 b 5.8. work consisted of strengthening cellar, and making dug out for signallers in barn, other work as above one man evacuated	TKK

2449 Wt. W14957/M90 750,000 1/16 J.B.C. & A. Forms/C.2118/12.

Army Form C. 2118.

Instructions regarding War Diaries and Intelligence Summaries are contained in F. S. Regs., Part II. and the Staff Manual respectively. Title pages will be prepared in manuscript.

WAR DIARY
or
INTELLIGENCE SUMMARY.
(Erase heading not required.)

Place	Date	Hour	Summary of Events and Information	Remarks and references to Appendices
	22/7/18.		Work commenced on construction of new Coy HQ at R 29 C 55.20, consisting of two elephant shelters, other work as above.	TKK
	23/7/18		Work as above, additional working party on BLUE LINE of 1½ Coys PIONEERS. This work shelled at night causing some casualties to working party. One man discharged from hospital	TKK
	24/7/18		Repairing of screen on CANTA CORNER, LE ROSSIGNOL road through R 19 & 20 commenced, other work as above & working parties same.	TKK
	25/7/18		One OR transferred to 476th Field Coy RE, one OR on leave to UK. Two OR wounded. Erection of baby elephant shelters in support line commenced, other work as above, No of men working on support line 600	TKK
	26/7/18		Two OR wounded 25/8 remained at duty, work as above, work on BLUE LINE hindered by lack of wiring materials and rain	TKK
	27/7/18		Two OR admitted to hospital, one OR evacuated, work & working parties as above	TKK
	28/7/18		Gas proofing of coy HQ at X 5 C 5.1 commenced and completed except for hanging blankets, other work as above	TKK
	29/7/18		Work as above, No of pioneers working on BLUE LINE reduced to 3 Platoons, total men employed on BLUE LINE 400, one OR on leave to UK.	TKK

A5834 Wt. W4973/M687 750,000 8/16 D. D. & L. Ltd. Forms/C.2118/13.

Instructions regarding War Diaries and Intelligence Summaries are contained in F. S. Regs., Part II. and the Staff Manual respectively. Title pages will be prepared in manuscript.

Army Form C. 2118.

WAR DIARY
or
INTELLIGENCE SUMMARY.
(Erase heading not required.)

Place	Date	Hour	Summary of Events and Information	Remarks and references to Appendices
	30/7/18		Work as above, progress better as weather conditions much improved	TKK
	31/7/18		Work as above, working parties same, site reconnoitred for O.P. for R.F.A.	TKK

H Gooch Major RE
O.C. 121 Field Coy R.E.

A5834 Wt. W4973/M687 750,000 8/16 D. D. & L. Ltd. Forms/C.2118/13.

VR 35

<u>Confidential</u>

War Diary. 121st Field Company R.E.

1st to 31st August 1918

Instructions regarding War Diaries and Intelligence Summaries are contained in F. S. Regs., Part II. and the Staff Manual respectively. Title pages will be prepared in manuscript.

WAR DIARY
or
INTELLIGENCE SUMMARY.
(*Erase heading not required.*)

121st Field Coy RE

Army Form C. 2118.

Place	Date	Hour	Summary of Events and Information	Remarks and references to Appendices
	1/8/18		Work as usual. Working parties same less one Coy on BLUE LINE owing to relief. Capt Knox relieved Major Gooch in evening. One man admitted to hospital. One man discharged hospital + one man evacuated.	WB
	2/8/18		Major Gooch proceeded to restcamp. Part of No 3 section relieved by No 2 on BLUE LINE and KORVE FARM. Heavy rain all day. Work started in Coy HQ at X 6 c 7 9 + X 11 a 4 3. Two O.R admitted to hospital. One O.R wounded. Two O.R proceed on leave	WB
	3/8/18		Work as above, working parties same. Work on BLUE LINE hindered by shell fire. Commenced at X 4 b 06 45 on O.P. Working party 7 men from 173 Bde. No 3 + 4 sections relieved each other. Switch from X 4 b 25 to R 34 d 5 2 commenced on BLUE LINE. One O.R proceeded on course at X Corps Lewis Gun School MERCKEGHEM. 2 O.R admitted into hospital. 2 O.R discharged from hospital	WB
	4/8/18		Work + parties on BLUE LINE the same. 11 Lt Davies + Cpl Crawford rejoined Coy from Course at ROUEN. 1 O.R proceeded on leave to U.K	WB
	5/8/18		Nos 1 + 2 Sections changed over work. Work as usual. 1 O.R admitted to hospital. 11 Lieut Delahey admitted to hospital	WB
	6/8/18		Work as above. Sergt King proceeded to ROUEN for Field Works Course	WB
	7/8/18		Work on BLUE LINE + Bde H.Q. hindered by shelling. A C.T from BLUE LINE to Support Line was reconnoitred. 1.O.R proceeded on leave to U.K.	WB
	8/8/18		Work with artillery same as before. Work on BLUE LINE same as above. Work hindered by shelling	WB
	9/8/18		Work on A battery B.C. post hindered by shelling. Work commenced on C.T from BLUE LINE to front line. 11 Lieut Delahey evacuated to CCS on 6/8/18	WB

D. D. & L., London, E.C.
(10340) Wt W3300/P713 750,000 5/15 E 2888 Forms/C2118/16

131st Field Coy RE

Army Form C. 2118.

Instructions regarding War Diaries and Intelligence Summaries are contained in F. S. Regs., Part II. and the Staff Manual respectively. Title pages will be prepared in manuscript.

WAR DIARY
or
INTELLIGENCE SUMMARY.

(Erase heading not required.)

Place	Date	Hour	Summary of Events and Information	Remarks and references to Appendices
	10/8/18		Work stopped on on 3a 4 + 12 artillery jobs Two NCO No 2 Section wounded work on rest of jobs same 15th R.I.R took over work on BLUE LINE + CT to front line	
	11/8/18		Two Coys only working on BLUE LINE work on other jobs same as above No work on C.T owing to infantry working parties bathing	
	12/8/18		Two Coys only working on BLUE LINE owing to bathing + other work the same 470000 C.S.M. Brown transferred to R.E.B.D. Rouen authority G.R. No 51307/178/Ca/7 7/18	
	13/8/18		Heavy gas shelling on SCHAEXKEN CORNER no work done at left of Blue line work started on ambulance relay post at LA MANCHE FARM working party supplied by RAMC. 3 O.R proceeded on leave to U.K 1 O.R discharged hospital	
	14/8/18		Work as above two Coys only on BLUE LINE owing to casualties on previous night from gas	
	15/8/18		Work on BLUE LINE + C.T to front trench parties same Right Coy temporary H.Q completed 4 OR to hospital 1 OR rejoined unit from Base	
	16/8/18		Work BLUE LINE + C.T same as above 12th R.I.R supplied 3 Coys for work 2 O.R proceeded to 2nd Army Rest Camp One O.R. to hospital	
	17/8/18		Work as above 4 O.R to hospital 2 ORs discharged hospital Five men per section were sent to Horse lines to be trained under a Cpl Lewis gun instructor from 107 Bgde	
	18/8/18		Work as above concreting of floor in the A.D.S finished work started on chamber for cook house. One O.R proceeded to U.K on reengagement leave	
	19/8/18		BLUE LINE + C.T work same Started enlarging Bgde H.Q dugout at PIEBROUCK. Water was struck in the northern entrance + work stopped a gallery was started opposite Southern entrance Pioneers changed for working party supplied by Bgde Pioneers put on C.T cleaning up & duck boarding	

D. D. & L., London, E.C.
(10340) Wt W3300/P713 750,000 5/18 E 2688 Forms/C2118/16

Instructions regarding War Diaries and Intelligence Summaries are contained in F. S. Regs., Part II. and the Staff Manual respectively. Title pages will be prepared in manuscript.

WAR DIARY
or
INTELLIGENCE SUMMARY.
(*Erase heading not required.*)

121st Field Co RE

Army Form C. 2118.

Place	Date	Hour	Summary of Events and Information	Remarks and references to Appendices
	20/8/18		Work on BLUE LINE + C.T same working parties 1 Coy 9th R I R + 2½ Coys 12th R I R pioneers away fatigue 2 O.R. evacuated 2 O.R. discharged hospital 1 O.R admitted hospital	[illegible]
	21/8/18		Work as above One O.R proceeded on Lewis Gun Course	[illegible]
	22/8/18		Work as above only one Coy + no pioneers on Blue line + C.T. One O.R discharged hospital	[illegible]
	23/8/18		Work as above 3½ Coys of infantry on C.T + BLUE LINE Two demolition charges at R 19 b 5 9 + Q 30 c 15 50 taken over from 255 Tunnelling Coy + 171 Tunnelling Coy 3 O.R proceeded on leave to U.K 1 O.R admitted to hospital	[illegible]
	24/8/18		Work on C.T + Blue line same working parties 1½ Coys other work same Two O.R admitted hospital One O.R discharged hospital	[illegible]
	25/8/18		A D S finished ready for occupation 1½ Coys employed on C.T + Blue line work hindered by heavy rain Started getting materials on site for gas proofing	[illegible]
	26/8/18		test points on buried Cable One OR admitted hospital one OR discharged Mules 48 cleared from horse lines field Work as above 3 OR admitted to hospital	[illegible]
	27/8/18		No working parties work as above carried on by sappers work started gas proofing test points at R 15 b 8 6 + R 16 d 6 6	[illegible]
	28/8/18		Work started by La MANCHE on 21 elephant to A D S stretcher cases Work as above no working parties Test points gas curtains finished 4 O.R. proceed on leave to U.K One O.R admitted to hospital	[illegible]
	29/8/18		The 204 Field Coy 35th Division looked over the work + all billets except the H Q at M de Cats R 19 b 3 7 One O.R discharged hospital	[illegible]

D. D. & L., London, E.C.
(10340) Wt W3300/P713 750,000 5/18 E 2688 Forms/C2118/16

Army Form C. 2118.

Instructions regarding War Diaries and Intelligence Summaries are contained in F. S. Regs., Part II. and the Staff Manual respectively. Title Pages will be prepared in manuscript.

WAR DIARY
or
INTELLIGENCE SUMMARY

(Erase heading not required.)

121st Field Co RE

Place	Date	Hour	Summary of Events and Information	Remarks and references to Appendices
	30/8/18		The relief by 204 Field Coy was cancelled in afternoon on account of enemy retiring. Sections standing by. Rear H.Q. with all transport moved to farms in area Sheet 27 P.33.a.95.25 arriving at 12.45 p.m. at 5.30 p.m. orders received to return to old location at Q.32.b.7.7. move completed at 7.15 p.m. One O.R admitted to hospital. Two O.Rs discharged from hospital. One Reinforcement from Base.	HRD
	31/8/18		Sections standing by. No. 4 Section moved to Coy. H.Q. billets. The pontoon was awarded first prize at Corps Horse Show. 2/Lt. Delahey rejoined unit from R.E.B.D. Rouen. One O.R. transferred to Base. 3 O.Rs on leave to U.K. One O.R evacuated & 2 O.Rs discharged hospital.	HRD

T.K. Kune
Capt RE
for O.C. 121st Fld. Co. R.E.

2449 Wt. W14957/M90 750,000 1/16 J.B.C. & A. Forms/C.2118/12.

Confidential

War Diary

of

121st Field Company RE

From 1-9-18 to 30-9-18

Instructions regarding War Diaries and Intelligence Summaries are contained in F. S. Regs., Part II. and the Staff Manual respectively. Title Pages will be prepared in manuscript.

WAR DIARY
or
INTELLIGENCE SUMMARY
(Erase heading not required.)

Army Form C. 2118.

Place	Date	Hour	Summary of Events and Information	Remarks and references to Appendices
	1.9.18		Transport lines moved to SCHAEXKEN – BERTHEN Road R28b3.6, horses in open and men in bivouack shelters. QMS stores moved to R28b6.4. No 1 & 2 sections moved to R35c 50.95 HQ to R19b3.7. 2OR proceeded to 2nd Army Rest Camp. 1OR evacuated.	TKK
	2.9.18		HQ & sec 3 & 4 moved to R35c 50.95	TKK
	3.9.18		2 sections employed clearing a space for RE dumps in St. Jeans Cappel, one section fixing up billets, one on horse lines. One O.R. discharged from hospital.	TKK
	4.9.18		Nos 1 & 3 sections employed on screening BRANDHTRE – NEUVE EGLISE ROAD. No 4 section fixing up cellar at S4b33. for an A.D.S. One OR rejoined unit from RE Training Centre	TKK
	5.9.18		Work as above, OC & 2nd in command reconnoitred for new billets between NEUVE EGLISE and BAILLEUL, 3OR proceeded on leave to UK.	TKK
	6.9.18		Transport employed on moving RE stores from St Jeans Capel to S4 b.1.8 (New RE dump in BAILLEUL) Nos 1 & 3 on screening, No 4 on ADS No 2 on loading RE stores and camp improvement. 1 OR proceeded to Field Works course in ROUEN.	TKK
	7.9.18		Completed move of RE stores to S4 b1.8 work as above one OR proceeded on leave to UK. 1OR discharged hospital.	TKK
	8.9.18		Work as Above	TKK
	9.9.18		Transport lines moved to TANILLA FARM R36 a.3.5. One section employed fixing up Div HQ in ST Jeans Capel, rest of sections on billets & H.Q.	TKK
	10.9.18		Two sections on screening, rest repairing billets etc	TKK
	11.9.18		No 1 & 2 sections moved to T14 c 8.7 Sheet 27. under bivouack sheets in old Nissen camp	TKK

2149 Wt. W14957/M90 750,000 1/16 J.B.C. & A. Forms/C.2118/12.

Army Form C. 2118.

Instructions regarding War Diaries and Intelligence Summaries are contained in F. S. Regs., Part II. and the Staff Manual respectively. Title Pages will be prepared in manuscript.

WAR DIARY
or
INTELLIGENCE SUMMARY

(Erase heading not required.)

Place	Date	Hour	Summary of Events and Information	Remarks and references to Appendices
	11.9.18		No 3 section demolishing dangerous walls in St Jeans Capel, 10 men screening Dranoutre – Neuve Eglise Road, rest of No 4 are on Div HQ. 2 OR proceeded on leave to UK.	TKK
	12.9.18		Work started on ADS on NEUVE EGLISE – WULVERGHEM RD. 28 SW/T 9 d 3.1 to consist of 1.18' Calais & 2.12' Calais shelters 4.2 proof, and on Support Batt HQ at UGBROOKE Farm T 10 c 90.90. Two Calais shelters 4.2 proof are being put in and a concrete shelter at present there being improved. Working parties 1 platoon by night & 9 men by day.	TKK
			New Bde HQ started at T 14 c 8.8. Three 12' Calais shelters 4.2 proof are to be built at present and extended afterwards to take POTTER GROUP HQ and one Nissen hut is being fitted up for a mess. Two OR admitted to hospital. Working parties 1 platoon in morning and afternoon.	
	13.9.18		Work as above. Marked out a line of posts to join up outposts between posts at U 13 b 2.8 and U 7 d 8.5.	TKK
	14.9.18		Established forward dumps at T 16 b 5.8, set out continuous trench to join up U 13 b 2.8 & U 7 d 8.5, and arranged to dig it through same night, owing to working parties not getting shovels only 200 yards of it completed. Work started on Reserve Bde HQ at T 15 b 3.6. to consist of Calais shelters dug in under old Nissen huts of Sankhill Camp, & made 4.2 proof. Working parties ½ platoon. Other work as above. Heavy gas shelling in front of Neuve Eglise, a direct hit with gas shell being made on ADS. St Dennis came up at night to take over front line work, four sappers [illegible] making shelters in this area	TKK

2.49 Wt. W14957/M90 750,000 1/16 J.B.C. & A. Forms/C.2118/12.

Instructions regarding War Diaries and Intelligence Summaries are contained in F. S. Regs., Part II. and the Staff Manual respectively. Title Pages will be prepared in manuscript.

WAR DIARY
or
INTELLIGENCE SUMMARY
(Erase heading not required.)

Army Form C. 2118.

Place	Date	Hour	Summary of Events and Information	Remarks and references to Appendices
	15.9.18		Two forward sections relieved by two sections of the 150 Field Coy RE and moved back to SCHAEXKEN CORNER ?35 c 50.95. Thirteen men of No 1 [illegible] bathed and obtained new uniforms after being exposed to mustard gas shelling.	TKR
	16.9.18		Two sections from front works employed cleaning up equipment etc, other two sections making horse standings etc. 24 [illegible] forwarded to 9th Corps rest camp.	TKR TKR
	17.9.18		No 1 section inoculated, other sections on horse standings. Major Gooch returned from leave UK extended on medical grounds	HRD
	18.9.18		No 1 Section resting after inoculation No 2 3 & 4 Physical training, drill & Lewis gun instruction. Warning orders received to move tomorrow	HRD
	19.9.18		Company moved from 27 R 35 c 50.95 to (HQ & 1 & 2 Sections) 27 P 30 b 75.55 Horse lines & 3 & 4 Sections to 27 Q 25 a 65.95. One O.R admitted to hospital One O.R discharged hospital Four O.Rs on leave to U.K	HRD
	20.9.18		On night of 20th–21st Company moved by route march from 27 P 30 b 75.55 and 27 Q 25 a 65.95 to ESQUELBECQ 27 C 8 c 95.70	HRD
	21.9.18		Company on improving billets	HRD
	22.9.18		Physical training & standing by ready for move One O.R evacuated	HRD
	23.9.18		Capt Knox & 5 O.R visited the Navy at DUNKERQUE. Three O.Rs on leave to U.K	HRD

2449 Wt. W14957/M90 750,000 1/16 J.B.C. & A. Forms/C.2118/12.

Instructions regarding War Diaries and Intelligence Summaries are contained in F. S. Regs., Part II. and the Staff Manual respectively. Title Pages will be prepared in manuscript.

WAR DIARY
or
INTELLIGENCE SUMMARY

(Erase heading not required.)

Army Form C. 2118.

Place	Date	Hour	Summary of Events and Information	Remarks and references to Appendices
	24.9.18		The Company training 2 O.Rs admitted hospital	HKD
	25.9.18		The Company was inspected by the G O C Major General Coffin V.C. D.S.O. afterwards he presented medal ribbons won during the March retreat to Major Finch M.C. Capt. Knox M.C. + three O.Rs. M.M.	HKD
	26.9.18		The Company moved by march route on the night 26th–27th from ESQUELBECQ 27 C.11 c 95.70 to Scout Camp 27 F. 28 c 7.4. Horse lines to Ball Camp. Capt Knox + 3 O.Rs on leave to U.K. One O.R. injured (thrown from horse)	HKD
	27.9.18		Company moved from SCOUT CAMP 27 F 28 c 7–4 to TAYLOR CAMP 27 A 26 b 1.6. ~~[illegible]~~	HKD
	28.9.18		2 O.Rs proceeded to 2nd Army Rest Camp at Audruicq. Lt H R Dixon proceeded on leave to U.K. period 31-9-18. to 14-10-18. Offensive started by Belgian and British	AEA
	29-9-18		At 4-30 a.m. Company moved from TAYLOR CAMP. A26 b1.6. to H 12 d.5.2 (accommodation in the wood). At 2 p.m. Company moved from H 12 d.5.2 to REIGERSBURG CHATEAU H.6.b central. 3 O.Rs on leave to U.K. period 30-9-18 to 14-10-18. Lieut G. C. Shute and 2Lt W.A. Delahay reported back from leave in France	AEA
	30.9.18		1 Offr. and 20 cyclists proceeded to a Div.l H.Qrs. to work on bridges in newly captured area	AEA

J.H. Allan Capt RE
for O.C. 121 Field Coy R.E.

2449 Wt. W14957/M90 750,000 1/16 J.B.C. & A. Forms/C.2118/12.

CONFIDENTIAL

Vol 37

WAR DIARY for month of
October, 1918.

121st Field Coy., R.E.

Instructions regarding War Diaries and Intelligence Summaries are contained in F. S. Regs., Part II. and the Staff Manual respectively. Title pages will be prepared in manuscript.

WAR DIARY
or
~~INTELLIGENCE SUMMARY.~~
(Erase heading not required.)

Army Form C. 2118.

Place	Date	Hour	Summary of Events and Information	Remarks and references to Appendices
	1/10/18.		Company moved from REIGERSBERG CHATEAU (H6b central) to J12 C 9.5. One O.R. admitted hospital. Pontoon and trestle waggons, 6 O.R. remained at H6b central.	a.l.S.
	2/10/18.		Company employed on road repairs. 3 O.R.s on leave to U.K.	a.l.S.
	3/10/18.		Whole Company on road repair	a.l.S.
	4/10/18.		428573 Sergt. Price J. proceeded to England to join R.E. Cadet Bn at Newark for Commission	
	5/10/18.		Pontoons and trestle waggons, 6 O.R. moved from REIGERSBERG CHATEAU (H6b central) to J12 C 9.5. No1 Section on pontooning drill in afternoon 2 O.R.s evacuated	a.l.S.
	6/10/18.		No1 Section on Bridging Drill. No 2, 3, & 4 Sections on roads. 4 O.R.s on leave to U.K.	a.l.S.
	7/10/18		No 2 Section Bridging. Remainder of Company on roads. Horse lines moved to K.7.a.7.2.	a.l.S.
	8/10/18		No 3 Sect. Bridging. Remainder on roads.	a.l.S.
	9/10/18		5 O.R.s on leave to U.K. One O.R. evacuated. No 4 Section Bridging	a.l.S.
	10/10/18		2Lt. Davies proceeded on leave to U.K. One O.R. evacuated.	a.l.S.

D. D. & L., London, E.C.
(10340) Wt W3300/P713 750,000 5/18 E 2688 Forms/C2118/16

Instructions regarding War Diaries and Intelligence Summaries are contained in F. S. Regs., Part II. and the Staff Manual respectively. Title pages will be prepared in manuscript.

WAR DIARY
or
INTELLIGENCE SUMMARY.

(*Erase heading not required.*)

Army Form C. 2118.

Place	Date	Hour	Summary of Events and Information	Remarks and references to Appendices
10/10/18			1 Off. sent to reconnoitre TERHAND - VIJWEGEN roads. 5 Cyclists from 2 and 3 sections sent forward to repair road.	a.l.
11/10/18.			Company on Bridging, L.G. Training and Billet improvement. 1 Off. sent to report on material etc necessary for gas proofing Adv. Bde HQ at GUINNESS HOUSE K.17.d.5.3	a.l.
12/10/18.			4 ORs on leave to UK. 3 Cyclists to repair TERHAND - VIJWEGEN road. 6 Cyclists and limber sent forward to Gasproof Adv. Bde and Arty Bde HQs at (K.17.d.5.3). Remainder of Company on Bridging, L.G. Training and Billet improvement. 2 ORs proceeded to 2nd Army Rest Camp Auxi-le-Château. Capt T.K. KNOX returned from leave.	a.l.
13.10/18			Pontoon (two) loaded up with bridging material ready to move up	T.K.
14.10/18			1 OR proceeded on leave to UK. At 5.20 am [illegible] proceeded [illegible]. Dismounted sections and two [illegible] wagons with the [illegible] & pack mules moved forward at 10.30 to K.32 b.7.9 Sheet 28 N.E. At Zero + 3 hrs (25.40?) two sections moved forward to [illegible] roads at L.19 a 3.9 which they found [illegible] and cleared a way [illegible], and two sections proceeded to JOHN'S BRIDGE L.13.d 8.1 which they found [illegible]. Bridging wagons moved up to K.22 c 3.3. [illegible] [illegible] [illegible] [illegible] [illegible]. Coy billets [illegible] at L.22 c 5.3 (?)	T.K.

G.S.C. 1.9

D. D. & L., London, E.C. (10349) Wt W5300/P713 750,000 5/18 E 2688 Forms/C2118/16

Instructions regarding War Diaries and Intelligence Summaries are contained in F. S. Regs., Part II. and the Staff Manual respectively. Title pages will be prepared in manuscript.

WAR DIARY
or
INTELLIGENCE SUMMARY.
(Erase heading not required.)

Army Form C. 2118.

Place	Date	Hour	Summary of Events and Information	Remarks and references to Appendices
15/10/18			Road examined up to [illegible] 2 c 1.3 and found good.	
16/10/18			One section with one pontoon wagon carrying 5 infantry [illegible] moved up at 01.00 to G 13 d 4.3. two sections moved up to same place at 31.30. At zero hour 05.30 the section moved forward with infantry [illegible] [illegible] [illegible] [illegible] [illegible] [illegible] [illegible] [illegible] and [illegible] [illegible] for infantry [illegible]. The other two sections followed up with infantry [illegible] [illegible] [illegible] [illegible] [illegible] [illegible] [illegible] [illegible] [illegible] which were found to have been blown. Company moved [illegible]	TK
			POLLEYHEM CAPPELLE . L3.D2.3.	TK
17/10/18			Day spent cleaning up	TK
18/10/18			4 OR proceeded on leave to UK 1 OR previously reported [illegible] now reported died of wounds. Coy moved to 39 c 52. Sheet 29. [illegible] [illegible] line to A 23 c 1.9 Sheet 29. [illegible] [illegible] went forward and reconnoitred canal in square C 19 & 20 with view of bridging	
19/10/18			Pontoons moved up to A 24 d 2.9 and unloaded and hidden in farm building at that point at 2 a.m.	

D. D. & L., London, E.C.
(10340) Wt W5300/P713 750,000 5/18 E 2688 Forms/C2118/16

Instructions regarding War Diaries and Intelligence Summaries are contained in F. S. Regs., Part II. and the Staff Manual respectively. Title pages will be prepared in manuscript.

WAR DIARY
or
INTELLIGENCE SUMMARY.

(Erase heading not required.)

Army Form C. 2118.

Place	Date	Hour	Summary of Events and Information	Remarks and references to Appendices
19/10/18			The company proceeded to [illegible] where pontoons were stored at 18.00, and launched two boats. Two companies of infantry arrived at canal at 19.25 and were ferried across the canal by 20.15. The enemy opened heavy machine gun fire after the second boat had been taken across. Immediately the two coys were across a light pontoon bridge was thrown across. It was completed by 22.00, the enemy putting down a heavy gas and HE barrage on the canal during the operation [illegible] the company had 2 casualties. At 22.00 the 107 Infantry Bgde crossed over the bridge without casualties.	T.K.
20/10/18			At 2.00 two battalions of 107 Bde crossed. At 4.30 the enemy attacked [illegible] the bridge destroying one boat but not damaging the pontoons, this was immediately replaced. One Company [illegible] the 107 Infantry Brigade crossed by 7.00. In the afternoon a foot bridge was put across. [illegible] the pontoon bridge was dismantled one boat being used by the 150 Field Coy to complete the medium bridge they were building across. Company moved into billets at C.19 a.3.3. Sheet 29 N.W.	H.W.

D. D. & L., London, E.C.
(10340) Wt W3300/P713 750,000 5/18 E 2688 Forms/C2118/16

Army Form C. 2118.

WAR DIARY
or
INTELLIGENCE SUMMARY.
(Erase heading not required.)

Instructions regarding War Diaries and Intelligence Summaries are contained in F. S. Regs., Part II. and the Staff Manual respectively. Title pages will be prepared in manuscript.

Place	Date	Hour	Summary of Events and Information	Remarks and references to Appendices
21/10/18			Medium bridge [illegible] C 19 [illegible] [illegible]	T.R.K.
22/10/18			[illegible] at C 19 b 2 2 Four O R proceeded on leave to U K	T.R.K.
23/10/18			Work carried on [illegible] at C 19 b 2 [illegible] and approaches at C 19 b 4 [illegible]	T.R.K.
24/10/18			Medium bridge at C 19 b 2 2 completed [illegible] 1 O R proceeded on leave to U K. 1 O R rejoined from Base. 1 O R evacuated. 4 O R previously reported [illegible] now reported wounded (gassed)	T.R.K.

D. D. & L., London, E.C.
(10340) Wt W3500/P713 750,000 5/15 E 2688 Forms/C2118/16

Instructions regarding War Diaries and Intelligence Summaries are contained in F. S. Regs., Part II. and the Staff Manual respectively. Title pages will be prepared in manuscript.

WAR DIARY
or
INTELLIGENCE SUMMARY.
(Erase heading not required.)

Army Form C. 2118.

Place	Date	Hour	Summary of Events and Information	Remarks and references to Appendices
25 10/18			Medium bridge at C19 b.2.2 completed with approaches	
26 10/18			Company employed on improvement to roads leading to bridge at C19 b.2.2. 1 O.R. previously reported killed in action now reported died of wounds 19/10/18. 4 O.R. proceeded on leave to U.K. 3 O.R. came from base (reinforcements) 1 O.R. rejoined from base.	
27 10/18			Pontoon bridge gear at C19 b.4.2 checked and handed over to 34 Div R.E. equivalent gear being drawn from train. 1 O.R. admitted to hospital.	
28 10/18			Company moved with transport to S.27/M.2 & d.2.4. 5 O.R. evacuated – N.Y.D. gas.	
29 10/18			Company employed on overhauling pontoon gear & tool carts, & kit inspection.	
30 10/18			Company [illegible] [illegible] not [illegible] [illegible] in afternoon [illegible] [illegible] in bad [illegible]	
31 10/18			[illegible] [illegible] of making [illegible] bridge [illegible] [illegible] Company [illegible] general training and [illegible] [illegible] proceeded to a course on instruction in horse management. 5 O.R. on leave to U.K.	

[illegible] Major. R.E.
O.C. 121st Field Coy. R.E.

D. D. & L., London, E.C.
(10340) Wt W3300/P713 750,000 5/18 E 2688 Forms/C2118/16

CONFIDENTIAL

VR 38

121st Field Co. R.E.

WAR DIARY for month of Novr. 1918.

121ST
FIELD COMPANY,
R.E.
No. M162
Date 30/12

Instructions regarding War Diaries and Intelligence Summaries are contained in F. S. Regs., Part II. and the Staff Manual respectively. Title pages will be prepared in manuscript.

WAR DIARY
or
INTELLIGENCE SUMMARY.
(Erase heading not required.)

Army Form C. 2118.

Place	Date	Hour	Summary of Events and Information	Remarks and references to Appendices
1.11.18			The following awards were received for gallantry and devotion to duty during the recent operations.	TKR
			57607 2nd Cpl W G Gowdy awarded bar to M.M. for conspicuous gallantry when in charge of a party carrying up material to bridges over L[illegible] under heavy fire	
			No 65402 Sgt R H King; 57774 A/Cpl W T McKnight; 420278 Cpl McClean E; 6412 L/Cpl [illegible]; 413671 " Gibb G; 103086 Pte McConnell; 479978 " Nelson [illegible]; 6442 " Marshall; 57633 L/Cpl McFadden D — Awarded M.M. for conspicuous gallantry when building a bridge across the river L[illegible] under heavy fire	
			57478 L Cpl Moore J. Awarded M.M. for conspicuous gallantry in taking their pontoon wagons loaded with bridging material through a heavy barrage to repair a bridge at [illegible].	
			Company doing general training and route marching.	

D. D. & L., London, E.C.
(10340) Wt W5300/P713 750,000 5/18 E 2688 Forms/C2118/16

Instructions regarding War Diaries and Intelligence Summaries are contained in F. S. Regs., Part II. and the Staff Manual respectively. Title pages will be prepared in manuscript.

WAR DIARY
or
INTELLIGENCE SUMMARY.
(Erase heading not required.)

Army Form C. 2118.

Place	Date	Hour	Summary of Events and Information	Remarks and references to Appendices
1.11.18			Cpl Adams D. rejoined from leave and posted to No 3 Section. A/L/Cpl Jones [illegible] attached [illegible]	[illegible]
2.11.18			Company doing general training and experimenting with floating bridges [illegible] Cpl [illegible]	[illegible]
3.11.18			Company moved to [illegible] [illegible] rejoined from leave	[illegible]
4.11.18			Company doing general training and experimenting with floating bridges. [illegible] Cpl Rollaston [illegible] Proceeded on leave to U.K. [illegible] Spr [illegible] Cpl [illegible] attached to [illegible] for duty Cpl [illegible] Pte [illegible] Rejoined from leave [illegible] Cpl [illegible] Rejoined for duty from C.R.S.	[illegible]

D. D. & L., London, E.C.
(10340) Wt W5300/P713 750,000 5/15 E 2888 Forms/C2118/16

Instructions regarding War Diaries and Intelligence Summaries are contained in F. S. Regs., Part II. and the Staff Manual respectively. Title pages will be prepared in manuscript.

WAR DIARY
or
INTELLIGENCE SUMMARY.
(Erase heading not required.)

Army Form C. 2118.

Place	Date	Hour	Summary of Events and Information	Remarks and references to Appendices
5-11-18			Company on general training.	
			No 170863 Sp Champion [illegible] Rejoined Coy from [illegible]	
			164833 Sp [illegible] J } Rejoined from leave to UK	[illegible]
			50256 Pte Barnes A J }	
6-11-18			As above	
			93978 Sp Martin J rejoined from leave	
			[illegible] Cpl [illegible] evacuated to [illegible] CCS [illegible]	
			The following reinforcements joined Coy [illegible]	
			[illegible] [illegible] Cooke J	
			511837 Sp [illegible] J H	
			170108 [illegible] W J	
			145432 [illegible] F	
			342547 [illegible]	
			51235 Bellamy S	
			492557 Spencer H	
			[illegible] Fleming J	
			519205 Hall R	
			519239 Hitches E J	
			519824 [illegible] G R	

D. D. & L., London, E.C.
(10340) Wt W5300/P713 750,000 5/18 E 2688 Forms/C2118/16

Instructions regarding War Diaries and Intelligence Summaries are contained in F. S. Regs., Part II. and the Staff Manual respectively. Title pages will be prepared in manuscript.

WAR DIARY
or
INTELLIGENCE SUMMARY.
(Erase heading not required.)

Army Form C. 2118.

Place	Date	Hour	Summary of Events and Information	Remarks and references to Appendices
6-11-18			[illegible] Fletcher H.K. 342831 [illegible] Watts A [illegible] Pike [illegible] 243136 [illegible] Jones F.C. [illegible] Holywell [illegible] [illegible] Phillips J [illegible] [illegible] J [illegible] [illegible]	
7-11-18			Company on general training T. 2 Lt [illegible] RE awarded M.C. for gallantry and devotion to duty in the field.	
8-11-18			The company bathed in the morning afterwards doing general training & had an [illegible] football match in afternoon [illegible] [illegible] admitted to hospital	

D. D. & L., London, E.C.
(10340) Wt W3300/P713 750,000 5/10 E 2688 Forms/C2118/16

Instructions regarding War Diaries and Intelligence Summaries are contained in F. S. Regs., Part II. and the Staff Manual respectively. Title Pages will be prepared in manuscript.

WAR DIARY
or
INTELLIGENCE SUMMARY

(Erase heading not required.)

Army Form C. 2118.

Place	Date	Hour	Summary of Events and Information	Remarks and references to Appendices
9-11-18			No 57464 Sp Jennings E evacuated company on general training	TRK
10-11-18			Company moved to S/29. r 8d (AUTRYVE) and attached to X Corps for work on bridges over canal	TRK
11-11-18			Work commenced on bridge to carry 10 ton axle load over canal at BOSSUYT. Armistice signed	TRK
12-11-18			Work as above	TRK
13-11-18			No 64487. Sp Taylor J.A, No 486569 Sp Fraser W, No 154213 Sp Wilson J.B proceeded on leave to UK No 57774 act-ii Cpl McKnight WT proceeded on course of instruction to RE bridging school Major Gooch H MC RE awarded DSO Capt Knox TK MC RE awarded bar to MC No 64082 Cpl Nicholls T awarded DCM	TKK
14-11-18			Work continued on bridge. act Cpl Porter (No 96084) admitted to hospital.	TRK

2149 Wt. W14957/M90 750,000 1/16 J.B.C. & A. Forms/C.2118/12.

Army Form C. 2118.

Instructions regarding War Diaries and Intelligence Summaries are contained in F. S. Regs., Part II. and the Staff Manual respectively. Title Pages will be prepared in manuscript.

WAR DIARY
or
INTELLIGENCE SUMMARY

(Erase heading not required.)

Place	Date	Hour	Summary of Events and Information	Remarks and references to Appendices
15-11-18			Bridge over canal at BOSSUYT opened for traffic	
			No 57464 Sp Jennings E rejoined from base, No 519941 Dr Hill A evacuated,	TKK
			The following reinforcements joined the company from the base	
			466942 Sp Sutcliffe CR	
			203179 " Godwin RH	
			400788 Dr Jones GW	
			83975 " Makinson J	
			612148 " Peirce H	
			52314 " Pearson J	
			488286 " Leavsley JT	
16-11-18			Company employed on cleaning up bridge site and strutting the bank, of canal	
			No 532114 Sp Richardson PJ proceeded on leave to UK	TKK
17-11-18			Work as above	TKK

2149 Wt. W14957/M90 750,000 1/16 J.B.C. & A. Forms/C.2118/12.

Army Form C. 2118.

WAR DIARY
or
INTELLIGENCE SUMMARY.
(*Erase heading not required.*)

Instructions regarding War Diaries and Intelligence Summaries are contained in F. S. Regs., Part II. and the Staff Manual respectively. Title pages will be prepared in manuscript.

Place	Date	Hour	Summary of Events and Information	Remarks and references to Appendices
	18/11/18		The Company moved to MOUSCRON	HRD
	19/11/18		Company employed in cleaning equipment &c Lecture by Commdr C B Spicer Simpson DSO RN Functions of Fleet & Anti submarine campaign. Places allotted to Coy for 3 officers & 23 O.R 1 Rider transferred to 9th Div 1 OR admitted Hospital 1 O.R rejoined from Base	HRD
	20/11/18		98619 Spr Holliday W.S transferred to H.Q.R.E 36th Div & apptd pd L/cpl with effect from 4/11/18 Men on General training	HRD
	21/11/18		Company on general training M.O's lecture at 11 a.m 277452 Spr Wyatt B.J granted special leave to U.K	HRD
	22/11/18		Company on general training 1 O.R rejoined Coy from Rest Camp 2 O.Rs evacuated	HRD
	23/11/18		Church Parade 9.45 a.m Lecture by Mr Young Husband on Exploration between Russia & India	HRD
	24/11/18		Coy on general training 2 O.R granted leave to U.K	HRD

D. D. & L., London, E.C.
(10340) Wt W3300/P713 750,000 3/15 E 2688 Forms/C2118/16

Instructions regarding War Diaries and Intelligence Summaries are contained in F. S. Regs., Part II. and the Staff Manual respectively. Title pages will be prepared in manuscript.

WAR DIARY
or
INTELLIGENCE SUMMARY.

(*Erase heading not required.*)

Army Form C. 2118.

Place	Date	Hour	Summary of Events and Information	Remarks and references to Appendices
	25/11/18		Full Marching order parade for O.C.s inspection 1 O.R evacuated 22476 Driver Collins B tried by F.G.C.M	HRD
	26/11/18		Coy on general training 1 OR granted leave to U.K Lecture by Lieut Walmsley at 5.00 Vacancies allotted 2 Officers + 8 O.R Subject Aircraft	HRD
	27/11/18		General training in morning Bathing Parade 2 pm	HRD
	28/11/18		General training + Inspection by M.O 22476 Driver Collins B Found guilty of absence without leave from 11/11/18 to 14/11/18 + sentenced to 21 days F.P. No 2 1 O.R rejoined Coy from Base	HRD
	29/11/18		Soldier Kiln started for 36th Divisional Salvage Coy Dismounted sections change billets One O.R admitted hospital Lecture on Demobilization + Reconstruction by Major D BORDEN TURNER 8 Seats allotted 64238 Sergt McRoberts H rejoined Coy from Base	HRD
	30/11/18		General training + sports One OR evacuated H Moore [illegible] RE 30/11/18 OC [illegible] Coy RE.	HRD

D. D. & L., London, E.C.
(10340) Wt W5300/P713 750,000 5/15 E 2688 Forms/C2118/16

CONFIDENTIAL

WAR DIARY
of
121 FIELD COMPANY - RE
for
DECEMBER - 1918

Army Form C. 2118.

Instructions regarding War Diaries and Intelligence Summaries are contained in F. S. Regs., Part II. and the Staff Manual respectively. Title pages will be prepared in manuscript.

WAR DIARY
or
INTELLIGENCE SUMMARY.
(*Erase heading not required.*)

Place	Date	Hour	Summary of Events and Information	Remarks and references to Appendices
1-12-18			C of E parade 9-20 a.m. Non conformist 10-30 a.m.	TKR
2-12-18			Company employed on general training, with details working on refuse destructor for town major, soldier billets etc.	TKR
			57640 Spr Mulhall J.J. } leave to U.K.	
			80593 Lt Russell W. }	
			Lecture by Col Swinyne RE on "Exploration" in afternoon	
3-12-18			Parades & work as above	TKR
			209216 Dr Dow S. commended on 30-11-18	
			Lecture by Capt A. Bees on [illegible] the Great War	
			391399 S/o Whittaker [illegible] tried by F.G.C.M. for absence without leave 2/11/18–12/11/18	
4-12-18			Work & parades as above in morning, company bathed in afternoon	
			49919 a/Sgt Peterson W. proceeded on leave to U.K.	
			57774 a/L/Cpl McKnight rejoined from RE Bridging school	TKR
			543[illegible] a/L/Cpl Kirk E.J. appt. a/Cpl from 22/11/18 vice 96084 a/Cpl Pater C. [illegible]	
			57676 2a/Cpl Gilmore R.J. [illegible] a/L/Cpl from 22/11/18	
			57765 Sr a Kane appt L/Cpl (pd) from 4/12/18	
			Lecture by Capt. Bewlee on night bombing in Hadley Prue	
				TKR

D. D. & L., London, E.C.
(10340) Wt W3300/P713 750,000 5/15 E 2688 Forms/C2118/16

Instructions regarding War Diaries and Intelligence Summaries are contained in F. S. Regs., Part II. and the Staff Manual respectively. Title Pages will be prepared in manuscript.

WAR DIARY
or
INTELLIGENCE SUMMARY

(Erase heading not required.)

Army Form C. 2118.

Place	Date	Hour	Summary of Events and Information	Remarks and references to Appendices
6-12-18			Company paraded at 7-20 am and marched with four tool carts & 4 limbers to HALLUIN AERODOME, where a practice march past was held by division.	TKK
			396374 Sp Whittaker A sentenced to 42 days F.P. No 1. by F.G.C.M. for being absent without leave	
7-12-18			Company employed building refuse destructors, solder kiln, alterations to stage for "Merry Mauves" and fixing up billets.	TKK
			342831 Sp Watts H proceeded to 36 MT Coy at HALLUIN for course in fitting	
			154788 Sp Jackson W, 23128 Evans R, 23127 Acton F. } proceeded to 214 ATCo MENIN for course in carpentry	
			63379 a Cpl Rainbird HA., 57779 Dr Prentice A } proceeded on leave to UK	
			Lecture by Mr E.F. ALLEN on Anglo-American Relations	
8-12-18			Detachment of 33 sappers under Lt Potts proceeded to RONCQ to work under CRE 39 div on bridges at MENIN.	TKK.
			T/Lt H.R. Dixon RE awarded French Croix de Guerre a l'ordre Army (Palm) vide 36 Div R.O. dated 7/12/18	
			Church parades 8-30 C.E. 10-30 N.C. Played 16 R.I.R football in afternoon	

2449 Wt. W14957/M90 750,000 1/16 J.B.C. & A. Forms/C.2118/12.

Army Form C. 2118.

Instructions regarding War Diaries and Intelligence Summaries are contained in F. S. Regs., Part II. and the Staff Manual respectively. Title Pages will be prepared in manuscript.

WAR DIARY
or
INTELLIGENCE SUMMARY
(Erase heading not required.)

Place	Date	Hour	Summary of Events and Information	Remarks and references to Appendices
9-12-18			Work as above, 244317 S/s Davies J transferred to unit from 122 Fd Coy RE as from 22/4/18	TKL
10-12-18.			Work as above. 57740 L Cpl Mellor admitted hospital, company practised ceremonial parade 10-30 – 12-0	TKL
			57461 Sp Hutchinson proceeded to Transport Base Depo, Calais, Auth. 3rd Ech. Wire Ax 690 dated 9/12/18	TKL
11-12-18.			Company employed on general work round town, and fixing up billets	TKL
			203179 S/s Godwin RH / 21954 Pte Jackson J, 1st R. Inniskillings (attd) } proceeded to Heavy Repair Workshops Rouen for course in fitting & blk smith	
12-12-18			Company paraded 7-30 for divisional inspection which was cancelled work as above.	TKL
			166603 S/s Rennie admitted to hospital on 18/4/18 whilst on leave to UK	
			323553 L Cpl Wells, 353135 Pt Goddard, 353163 " Edwards, 304046 S/s Ashford, 466927 " Moore, 353217 Pt Sawyer, 430175 " Swift, 430114 " Armstrong, 326120 S/s Loftus } Joined unit from base	

2449 Wt. W14957/M90 750,000 1/16 J.B.C. & A. Forms/C.2118/12.

Army Form C. 2118.

Instructions regarding War Diaries and Intelligence Summaries are contained in F. S. Regs., Part II. and the Staff Manual respectively. Title Pages will be prepared in manuscript.

WAR DIARY
or
INTELLIGENCE SUMMARY

(Erase heading not required.)

Place	Date	Hour	Summary of Events and Information	Remarks and references to Appendices
13-12-18			Parades & work as above Lecture by Rev Studdart-Kennedy on Physical fitness in civil & military life	TPK
14.12.18			57464 Spr Jennings E admitted hospital Parades & work as above. 37793 Dr. Thompson R. proceeded to Miners concentration Camp LA MADELINE for disposal & struck off strength of Company 37740 L/Cpl Mellon H. discharged hospital	HRD
15.12.18			Parades & work as above T/Lieut a/Capt. J. K. Knox M C. proceeded on special leave to U.K. Period 16/12/18 – 30/12/18 authority XV Corps A.C.1/89 of 11.12.18	HRD
16.12.18			Ceremonial Parade of Coy. at HALLUIN. Inspected by XV Corps Commander. Coy. moved off at 7.45 a.m. Dress, Dismounted Musketry Order, haversack waterproof sheet carried on belt. Mounted portion: Dress. Bandoliers 100056 Pte. Barns A.T. admitted to hospital	HRD
17.12.18			Parades & work same as 16.12.18 32353 L/Cpl Wells F.H. } leave to U.K. period 18/12/18 – 1/1/19. 64441 Pnr. Boyd. D. }	HRD

2449 Wt. W14957/M90 750,000 1/16 J.B.C. & A. Forms/C.2118/12.

Army Form C. 2118.

WAR DIARY
or
INTELLIGENCE SUMMARY
(Erase heading not required.)

Instructions regarding War Diaries and Intelligence Summaries are contained in F. S. Regs., Part II. and the Staff Manual respectively. Title Pages will be prepared in manuscript.

Place	Date	Hour	Summary of Events and Information	Remarks and references to Appendices
18.12.18			Parades & work same as above	HRD
19.12.18			Parades & work as above 532114 Spr. Richardson P.J. admitted to Convalescent Hospital EASTBOURNE on 2/12/18 on short leave to U.K.	HRD
20.12.18			Parades & work same as above	HRD
21.12.18			154788 Spr. Jackson T.W.) Rejoined unit from 214th A.T. Co, R.E. Carpentry Course 231127 " Acton F. 231128 " Emmas R. } 52314 Dvr. Pearson J. proceeded on course of fitting in Loco works ST. ETIENNE	HRD.
22.12.18			Parade 9.15 am. C of E. & 10.15 am. Pres. for Divine Service	HRD
23.12.18			Co. employed on general work round town & fixing up billets	HRD
24.12.18			Co. employed as above 532114 Spr. Richardson P.J. struck off strength of Co. 2/12/18.	HRD.
25.12.18			Mounted section & Sappers had Xmas dinner together in recreation room at 13.00 hours. Turkey, Goose, & beer were provided out of the Co. Comforts fund.	HRD

2449 Wt. W14957/M90 750,000 1/16 J.B.C. & A. Forms/C.2118/12.

Army Form C. 2118.

Instructions regarding War Diaries and Intelligence Summaries are contained in F. S. Regs., Part II. and the Staff Manual respectively. Title Pages will be prepared in manuscript.

WAR DIARY
or
INTELLIGENCE SUMMARY

(Erase heading not required.)

Place	Date	Hour	Summary of Events and Information	Remarks and references to Appendices
26.12.18.			Check Parade 9.30. a.m. 57453. L/Cpl. Hamilton J. C. M.M. granted "Kings Leave" to U.K. 27/12/18 – 14/1/19 24270 Spr. Aughey R. leave to U.K. 27.12.18 – 10-9-19.	HRD
27.12.18.			Coy employed on work about the Town & making road to stables (such as making incinerators, repairing roofs to billets, fixing up rifle range &c.	HRD HRD.
28.12.18			Coy employed as above Lieut. A Shortt proceeded on leave to Paris. period 28/12/18 – 6/1/19.	HRD
29.12.18			Coy employed as above	
30.12.18			Coy employed as above 2nd Lieut. Potts proceeded on Special leave to U.K.	HRD
31.12.18			Coy employed as above Capt T.K. Knox. M.C. returned from leave	HRD

2:49 Wt. W14957/M90 750,000 1/16 J.B.C. & A. Forms/C.2118/12.

36

VR 40

CONFIDENTIAL

WAR DIARY

of

121 FIELD COMPANY - RE

for

JANUARY 1919

Army Form C. 2118.

Instructions regarding War Diaries and Intelligence Summaries are contained in F. S. Regs., Part II. and the Staff Manual respectively. Title pages will be prepared in manuscript.

WAR DIARY
or
INTELLIGENCE SUMMARY.
(Erase heading not required.)

Place	Date	Hour	Summary of Events and Information	Remarks and references to Appendices
	1-1-19		Company employed on general work for 107 Brigade & division	TKL
	2-1-19		S/p Loftus J proceeded to central workshops Tank Corps TENEUR for course in fitting, work as above	TKL
	3-1-19		Sections inspected by M.O at 11.30 hours, work as above,	TKL
			S/pr Phillips F J } proceeded on leave to U.K. 4-1-19 – 18-1-19 Dr McGreevy D }	
			S/p Jennings E } Struck off strength of Coy as from 20-12-18, having been admitted Pr Barnes A }	
			hospital 13-12-18 and 15-12-18 respectively	
			S/p Goode W A admitted to hospital today	
			Pr Boyd D rejoined from leave to UK.	
	4-1-19		Work as above	TKL
	5-1-19		Kit inspection dismounted sections	TKL
	6-1-19		Mounted section kit inspection, rest of coy general work in town	TKL
			S/p Holmes J } admitted to hospital Pr Edwards J A }	

D. D. & L., London, E.C.
(10340) Wt W3300/P713 750,000 5/15 E 2688 Forms/C2118/16

Instructions regarding War Diaries and Intelligence Summaries are contained in F. S. Regs., Part II. and the Staff Manual respectively. Title pages will be prepared in manuscript.

WAR DIARY
or
INTELLIGENCE SUMMARY.
(Erase heading not required.)

Army Form C. 2118.

Place	Date	Hour	Summary of Events and Information	Remarks and references to Appendices
	7-1-19		Work as above,	
			La Cpl McFadden D } proceeded to 36 Div MT Coy for course motor driving	THK
			Dr Montgomery W }	
			S/p Macdonald A " " " smiths work	
			2 Officers + 9 OR went to Miss Lena Ashwell's concert party	THK
	8-1-19.		S/p Pettifer proceeded to concentration camp LA MADELINE - prior to dispersal & is struck off strength of unit	
			Dr Rooney J } Joined unit from base	
			" Boyles J }	THK
	9-1-19		Coy on general work in town.	
			S/p Drummond D } proceeded to 36 MT Coy for course in fitting, brass	
			" Davis J } moulding & sign writing respec'y.	
			Dr Collins }	
	10-1-19		Work as above	THK
	11-1-19		The following proceeded to the concentration camp LA MADELINE prior to dispersal, & struck off strength of unit.	THK

D. D. & L., London, E.C.
(10340) Wt W3300/P713 750,000 5/15 E 2688 Forms/C2118/16

Instructions regarding War Diaries and Intelligence Summaries are contained in F. S. Regs., Part II. and the Staff Manual respectively. Title pages will be prepared in manuscript.

WAR DIARY
or
INTELLIGENCE SUMMARY.
(Erase heading not required.)

Army Form C. 2118.

Place	Date	Hour	Summary of Events and Information	Remarks and references to Appendices
	11-1-19		Sgt Smith W; Sp Penny D, Sp Norman H, Sp Sparkman J, Sp Staley F, Sp Crook T.	
			Sp Thatcher HW – leave to UK period 12-1-19 – 26-1-19	TRL
			Lce Cpl Marshall R proceeded to 14 Ordnance Mob. Workshops for Course in Blacksmithy.	
			S/CB. Brewer to agricul^e school WORTBECOURT for course in agriculture	
			Pr Edwards IA discharged hospital today.	
	12-1-19		Divine service at 9-45 hours	TRL
			Sp Scott B, Le Cpl Nellor H, Sp Stafford K, " Jackson TW, " Milner W } to LA MADELINE for dispersal	
			Sp Holmes J discharged from hospital	
			LcCpl Marshall R rejoined from course	TRL
	14-1-19		Coy on general work in town	
	15-1-19		" " " " "	TRL

D. D. & L., London, E.C.
(10340) Wt W3300/P713 750,000 5/15 E 2688 Forms/C2118/16

Instructions regarding War Diaries and Intelligence Summaries are contained in F. S. Regs., Part II. and the Staff Manual respectively. Title pages will be prepared in manuscript.

WAR DIARY
or
INTELLIGENCE SUMMARY.
(Erase heading not required.)

Army Form C. 2118.

Place	Date	Hour	Summary of Events and Information	Remarks and references to Appendices
	16.1.19		Coy on general work in town	
	17.1.19		Work as above, Dr Graham W proceeded on leave to UK. 18-1-19 — 1-2-19	TKL
				YWA
	18.1.19.		Animals inspected and classified by Maj. Horner AVC Spr Aston J proceeded to concent^n camp LA MADELINE 13-1-19 Spr Goode WA to hospital 3-1-19 evacuated	TKL
	19.1.19.		C of E service 9-45 am Pres do do 10-30 am	
			2/Cpl Crawford } Spr Roberts T } " Jones FE } to concentration camp LA MADELINE for dispersal	YWA
	20.1.19		Work as before 2/Cpl Gammell GO } Spr Hogg G } " Blackwell E } Parker CT } Shaw C } Ashford AW } Dawson T } Goss R } To concentration camp LA MADELINE for dispersal	TKL

D.D.&L., London, E.C. (10340) Wt W3300/P713 750,000 5/15 E 2688 Forms/C2118/16

Instructions regarding War Diaries and Intelligence Summaries are contained in F. S. Regs., Part II. and the Staff Manual respectively. Title pages will be prepared in manuscript.

WAR DIARY
or
INTELLIGENCE SUMMARY.
(Erase heading not required.)

Army Form C. 2118.

Place	Date	Hour	Summary of Events and Information	Remarks and references to Appendices
	21-1-19		Sp Irwin S (formerly of this unit, now serving with 11th Field Coy R E) Awarded M.S.M. vide London Gazette 18-1-19	PK.
	22-1-19		~~Sgt NC Bo~~ Sgt McInnes S, Cpl Robson W, L Cpl Paddison W, " Marshall R, Sp Arnold L, " Holmes J, " Jennings G, " Whittaker A, Pr Sawyer W G – to concentration camp LA MADELINE for disposal	
			Animals classified by remount officers for demobiln.	PK
	23-1-19		2nd Cpl Whelan J. leave to UK. period 24-1-19 – 7-2-19	
	24-1-19		L/Cpl Chesman M F app Cpl (pd)	
	25-1-19		Sp Emmons R discharged from hospital	

D. D. & L., London, E.C.
(10340) Wt W3300/P713 750,000 5/15 E 2688 Forms/C2118/16

Army Form C. 2118.

Instructions regarding War Diaries and Intelligence Summaries are contained in F. S. Regs., Part II. and the Staff Manual respectively. Title Pages will be prepared in manuscript.

WAR DIARY
or
INTELLIGENCE · SUMMARY
(Erase heading not required.)

Place	Date	Hour	Summary of Events and Information	Remarks and references to Appendices
	26-1-19.		Company employed on general work for division	VR
			T Lt. Hugh R Dixon proceeded to concentration camp La Madeline for dispersal	
			L/cpl Cooke G (unpaid) app Lc/cpl (paid) - 5-11-18 to complete establishment	
	27-1-19.		A/ Cpl Evans H, L/cpl Cooke G., " Bach J, Sp Acton F, " Symonds J, " Horsfield J, " Spencer H, " Richards R E. } proceeded to concentration camp for dispersal	VR
			Lt A C Shortt RE proceeded to RE bridging school MONCHY CAYEAUX.	

2149 Wt. W14957/M90 750,000 1/16 J.B.C. & A. Forms/C.2118/12.

Army Form C. 2118.

Instructions regarding War Diaries and Intelligence Summaries are contained in F. S. Regs., Part II. and the Staff Manual respectively. Title pages will be prepared in manuscript.

WAR DIARY
or
INTELLIGENCE SUMMARY.

(Erase heading not required.)

Place	Date	Hour	Summary of Events and Information	Remarks and references to Appendices
	28-1-19		Work as before Rr. Hanna R Sp Bell T " Breckon J W " Griffiths Pte Dixon J (2 R.I.F) } proceeded to concentration camp for dispersal	TKK
	29-1-19		Work as before. company bathed in morning Cpl Rymer W R Sp Hynes H " Richards R E } proceeded to concentration camp for dispersal II Cpl Porter J joined unit from No 3 C.C.S.	TKK
	30-1-19		Work as before Rifles on charge of company inspected by Lt Symonds Asst. Armourer, Fifth Army.	TKK
	31-1-19		Work as before.	TKK

T.K. Knox
Capt R.E.
O.C. 121st Field Coy. R.E.

A5834 Wt. W4973/M687 750,000 8/16 D. D. & L. Ltd. Forms/C.2118/13.

CONFIDENTIAL Vol 41

WAR DIARY
of
121 FIELD COMPANY - R.E.
for
FEBRUARY - 1919

Army Form C. 2118.

Instructions regarding War Diaries and Intelligence Summaries are contained in F. S. Regs., Part II. and the Staff Manual respectively. Title pages will be prepared in manuscript.

WAR DIARY
or
~~INTELLIGENCE SUMMARY~~.

(*Erase heading not required.*)

Place	Date	Hour	Summary of Events and Information	Remarks and references to Appendices
Field	1.2.19.		Strength of unit now 4 officers and 152 OR still billeted in MOUSCRON.	
			Sappers Hunter and Leyburn proceeded to concentration camp for demobilisation.	
			Sapper Goode rejoined unit from base.	
			Remainder being employed on repairs to billets & erection of huts for Bde [illegible]	H.G.
	2.2.19.		Work as above.	H.G.
	3.3.19.		Lieut A.C. SHORTT R.E. struck off strength.	H.G.
			Sappers CROUCH and Pte CARLISLE (1st R. Innis Fus) proceeded to concentration camp.	
	4.2.19.		Bathing of men carried out.	H.G.
	5.2.19.		Work as above	H.G.
	6.2.19.		Sappers BROWN N.W., Pioneer BOYD D., EDWARDS F.A. Drs HARRISON C., STEWART J and Pte COLLINS G (1st R. Innis Fus) proceeded to concentration camp.	H.G.
	7.2.19.		a/2nd Cpl GILMORE R.J, L/Cpl MOORE J Drs COLLINS B, PRENTICE A and Spr GLENN J. proceeded to concentration camp.	H.G.
			Sapr NELSON S ~~[illegible]~~ went on leave. Spr HARKIN admitted to hospital	
	8.2.19		Work as above.	H.G.
	9.2.19.		T/Lieut a/Capt T.K. KNOX M.C. R.E. proceeded to concentration camp.	H.G.
	10.2.19		Spr GARLAND R. proceeded to concentration camp. Dr STRANEX went on leave.	
			T/Lieut W.A. DELAHEY M.C. RE appointed a/Capt vice CAPT McILDOWIE demobilised	H.G.

D. D. & L., London, E.C.
(10340) Wt W5300/P713 750,000 5/18 E 2688 Forms/C2118/16

Instructions regarding War Diaries and Intelligence Summaries are contained in F. S. Regs., Part II. and the Staff Manual respectively. Title pages will be prepared in manuscript.

WAR DIARY

or

~~INTELLIGENCE SUMMARY~~.

(Erase heading not required.)

Army Form C. 2118.

Place	Date	Hour	Summary of Events and Information	Remarks and references to Appendices
Field	11.2.19.		Work as above	H.G.
	12.2.19.		Dr HARRISON awarded 28 days FP No 2 for damaging government property.	H.G.
	13.2.19.		Sgt MITCHELL G.E., Sgt McROBERTS, Cpl HOWARTH H.A., Cpl CHARMAN M.R. Spr CLARK W.E., HITCHES E.J., SCHOFIELD J.H. and Sgt BREWER T.P. proceeded to concentration camp.	H.G.
	14.2.19.		Spr McCLEMENTS proceeded on leave.	H.G.
	15.2.19.		Spr TAYLOR J.A. proceeded to concentration camp for demobilisation	H.G.
			Spr HENDRY J. appointed a/II Cpl. Spr FALGATE, McCLEAN and Dr PIERCE appointed L/Cpl.	H.G.
	16.2.19.		Spr IRVINE and Dr GRAHAM proceeded to concentration camp	H.G.
	17.2.19.		II Cpl McKNIGHT, L/Cpl McFADDEN, Spr SHANNON, JOHNSTON and Dr ANDERSON proceeded to concentration camp	H.G.
	18.2.19.		Dr CARSE proceeded on leave to U.K.	H.G.
	19.2.19.		Dr ARMSTRONG awarded 40 days FP No 2 by FGCM for theft.	H.G.
			Spr RIDDELL S. proceeded on leave to U.K.	H.G.

D. D. & L., London, E.C.
(10340) Wt W3300/P713 750,000 5/15 E 2688 Forms/C2118/16

Army Form C. 2118.

Instructions regarding War Diaries and Intelligence Summaries are contained in F. S. Regs., Part II. and the Staff Manual respectively. Title pages will be prepared in manuscript.

WAR DIARY
or
INTELLIGENCE SUMMARY.
(Erase heading not required.)

Place	Date	Hour	Summary of Events and Information	Remarks and references to Appendices
Frin	20/2/19		Sap. ALLISON, Pr WARWICK, L/Cpl KANE, Dr GORDON and Dr JOHNSTON proceeded to concentration camp	HG
	21/2/19		Sapr HOCKLEY Transferred to HQ. R.E. 1 Man struck off strength. 1 MAH.	HG
	22/2/19		Men employed on billet repairs.	HG
	23/2/19		II Cpl GLIDDE proceeded on leave to U.K.	HG
	24/2/19		Sapr Portland proceeded to concentration camp	HG
	25/2/19		4 men proceeded on leave 1 man admitted hospital	HG
	26/2/19		1 Man Transferred to CRE HQ	HG
	27/2/19		1 Man proceeded on leave.	HG
	28/2/19		work as usual	HG

H Goodchild RE
OC 1st Field Coy RE

D. D. & L., London, E.C.
(10340) Wt W3300/P713 750,000 3/15 E 2688 Forms/C2118/16

www.ingramcontent.com/pod-product-compliance
Lightning Source LLC
Chambersburg PA
CBHW080903230426
43664CB00016B/2716